Adult Coloring Book

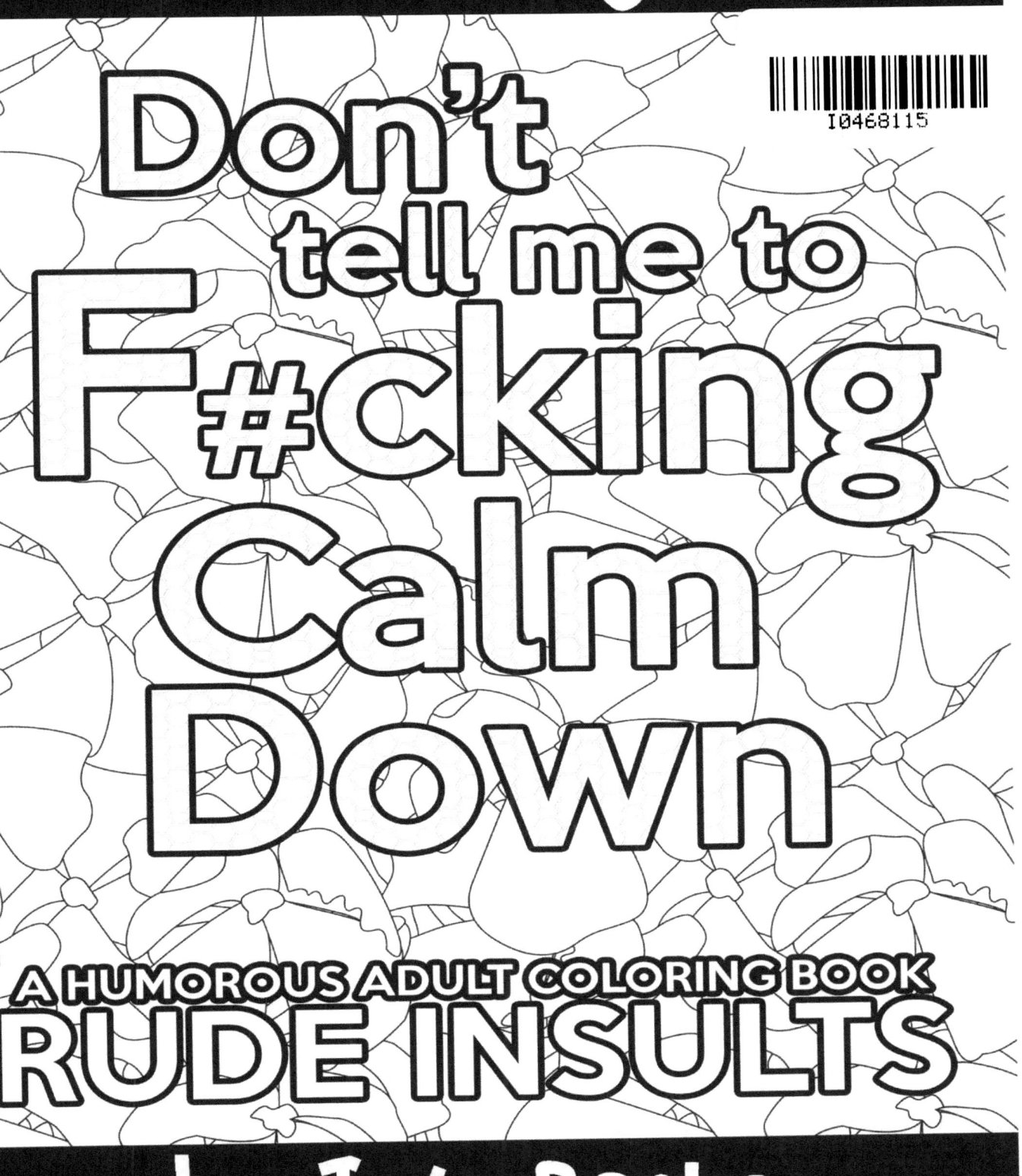

I0468115

Don't tell me to F#cking Calm Down

A HUMOROUS ADULT COLORING BOOK
RUDE INSULTS

by Jojo Banks

Warning:

Rude, crude and laugh out loud funny insults are contained within this awesome Adult Coloring Book and are meant for entertainment purposes only and are not intended to cause harm.

This Adult Coloring Book contains strong adult language and is not recommended for children.

At the end of the day, kick off your shoes, settle down and color in some rude and crude insults that would put you up to your neck in trouble if you ever uttered them out loud.

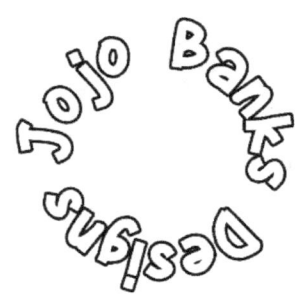

Stress Relief Coloring Books - Don't Tell Me To F#ucking Calm Down
By: Adult Coloring Books - Coloring Books for Grownups - Jojo Banks Designs
Copyright Jojo Banks Designs

ISBN-13: 978-1530058938

ISBN-10: 1530058937

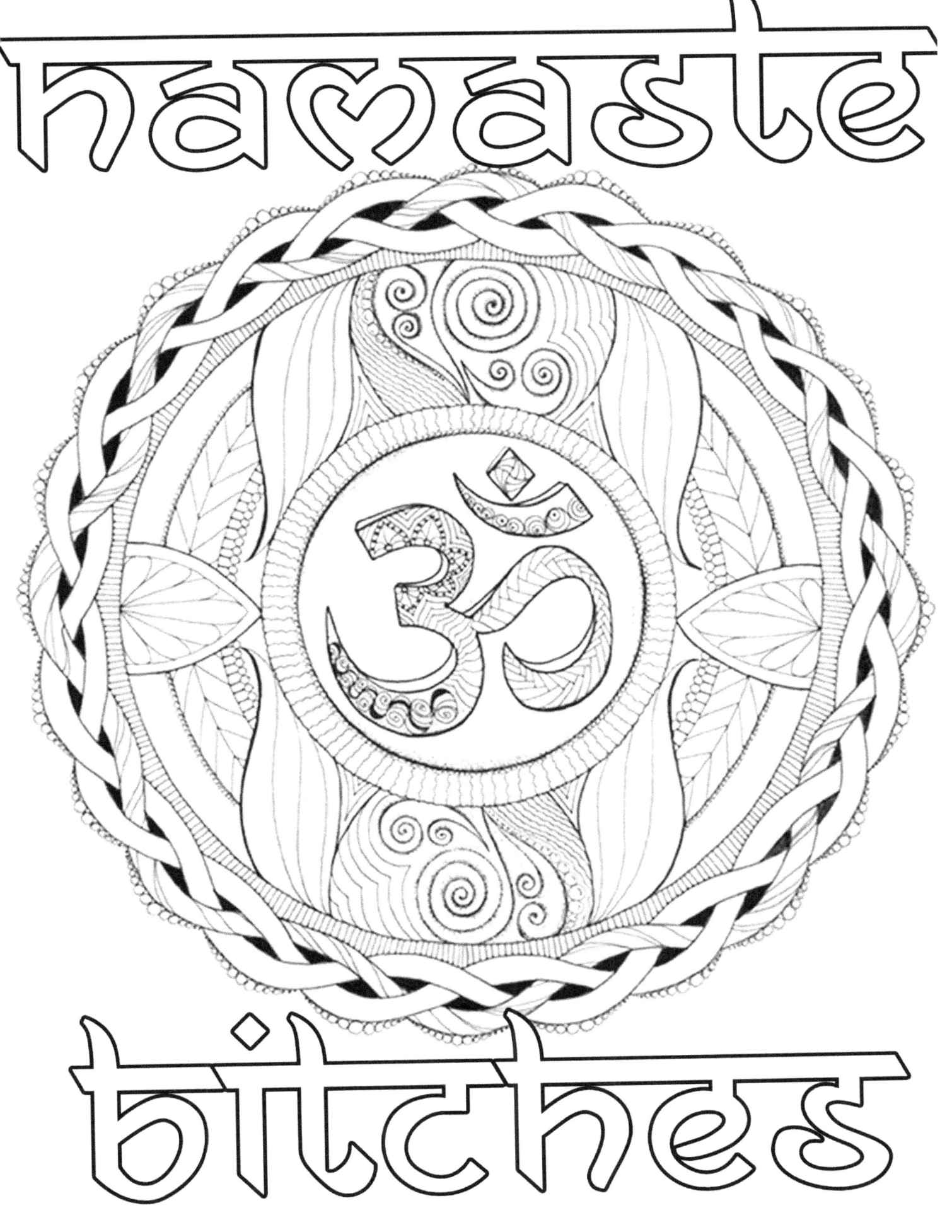

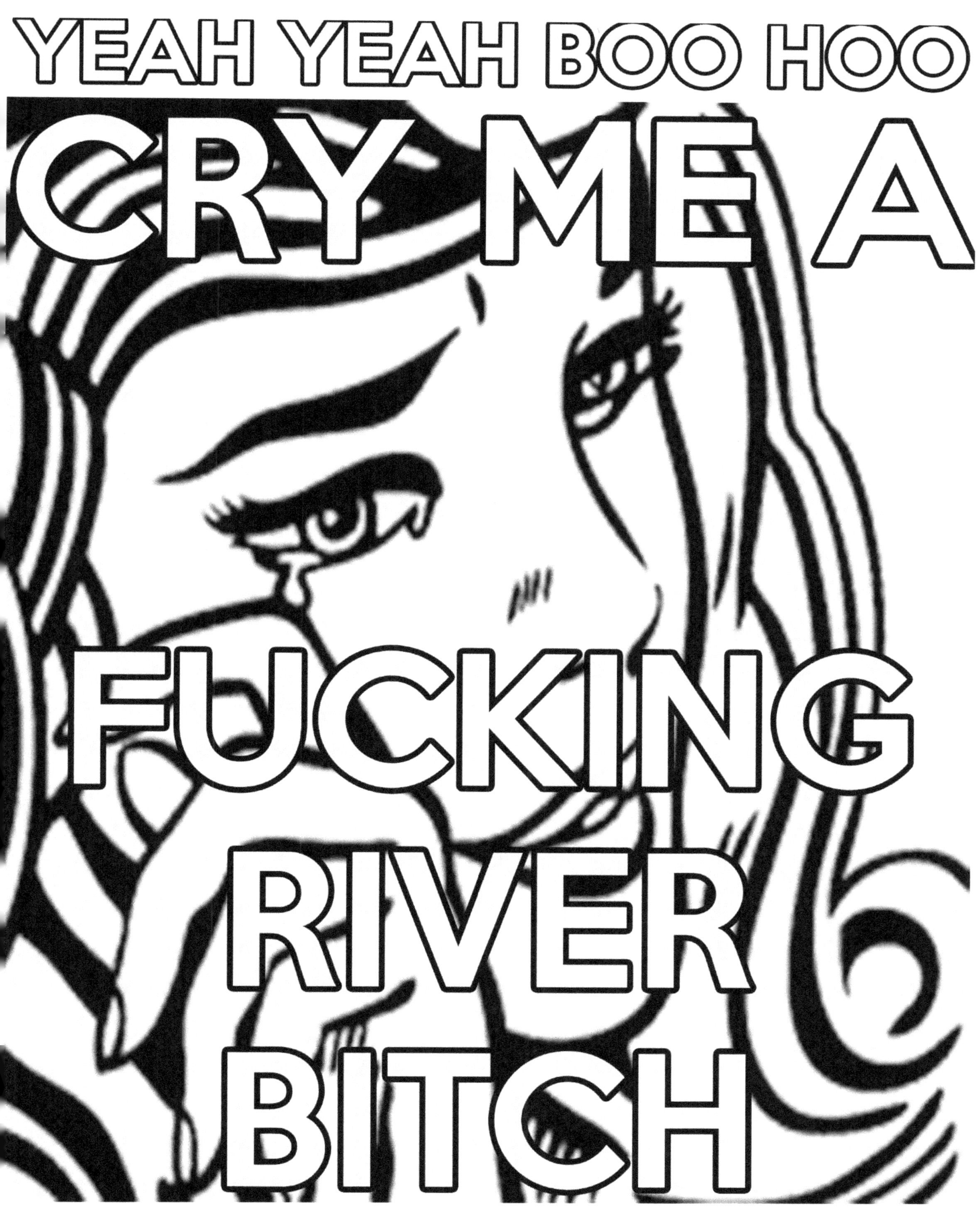
YEAH YEAH BOO HOO
CRY ME A
FUCKING
RIVER
BITCH
BOO HOO BOO HOO BOO HOO BOO HOO

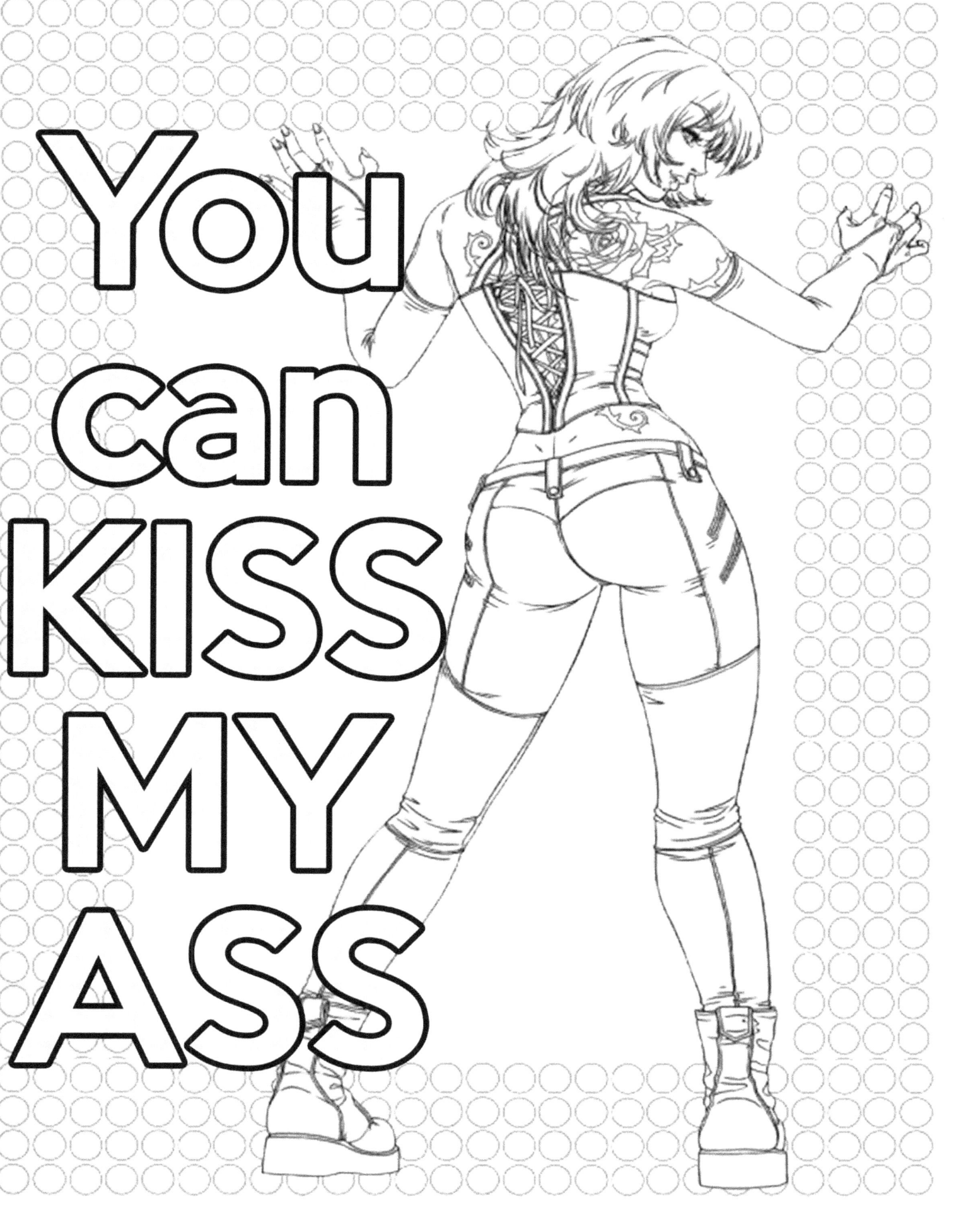

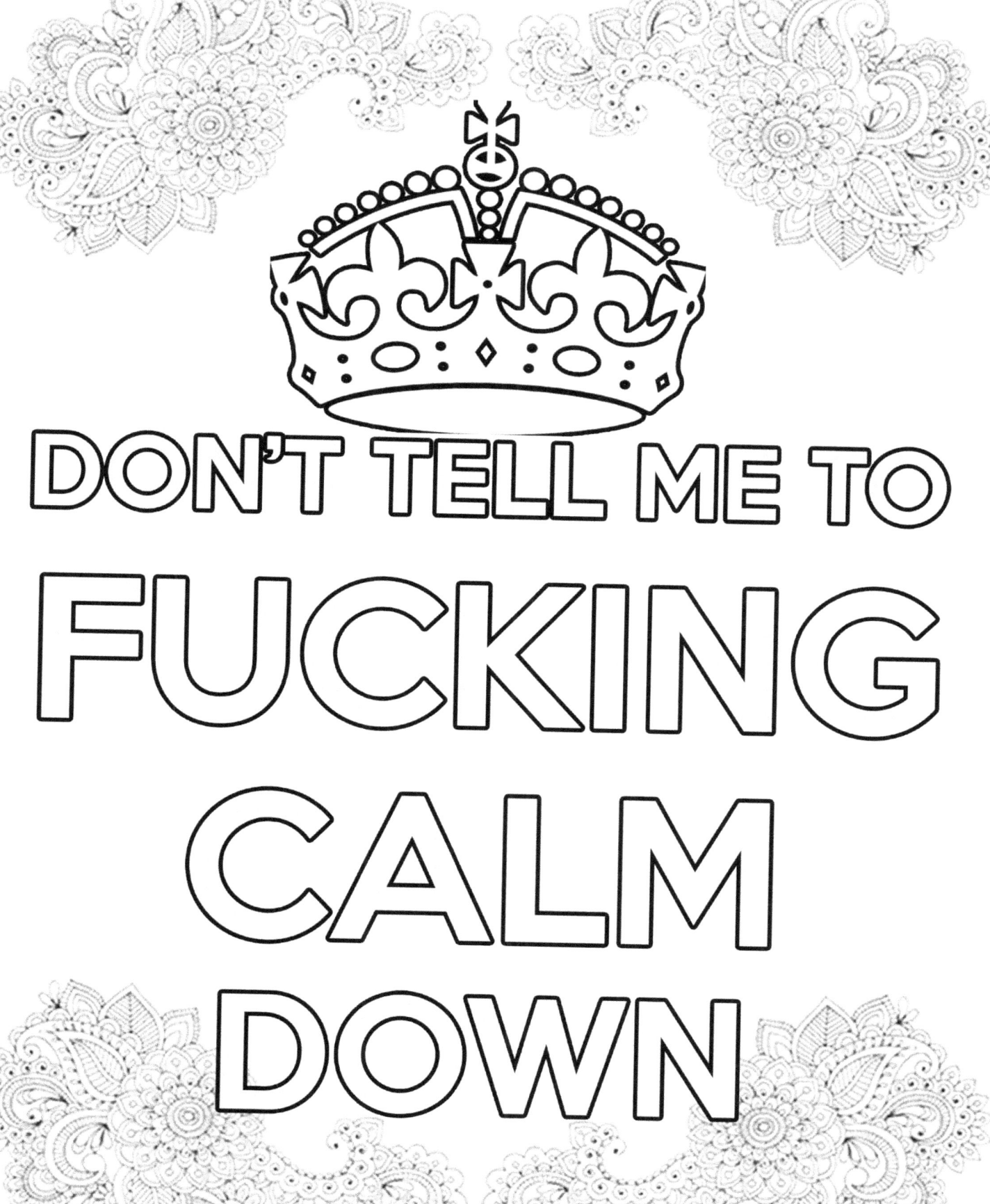

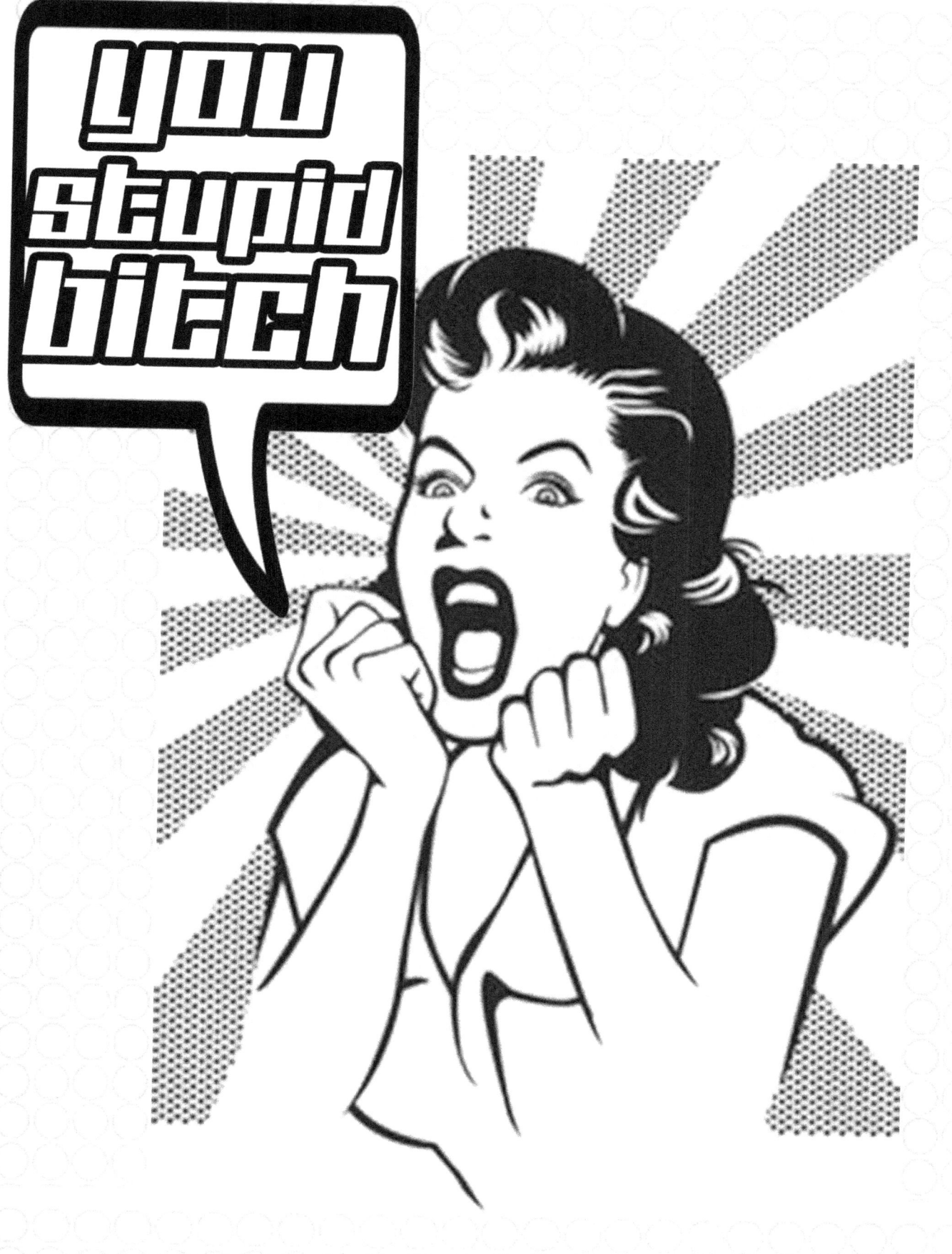

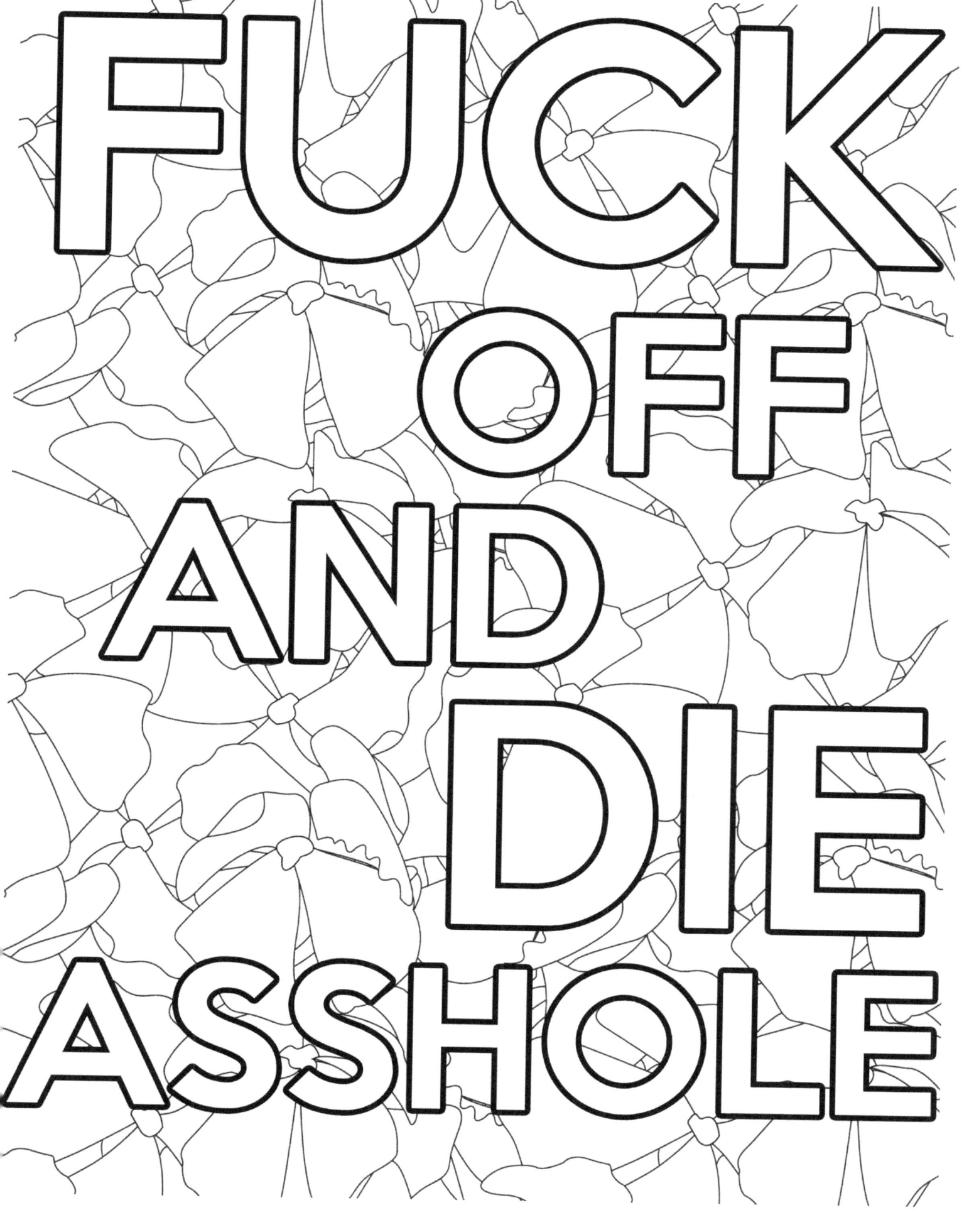

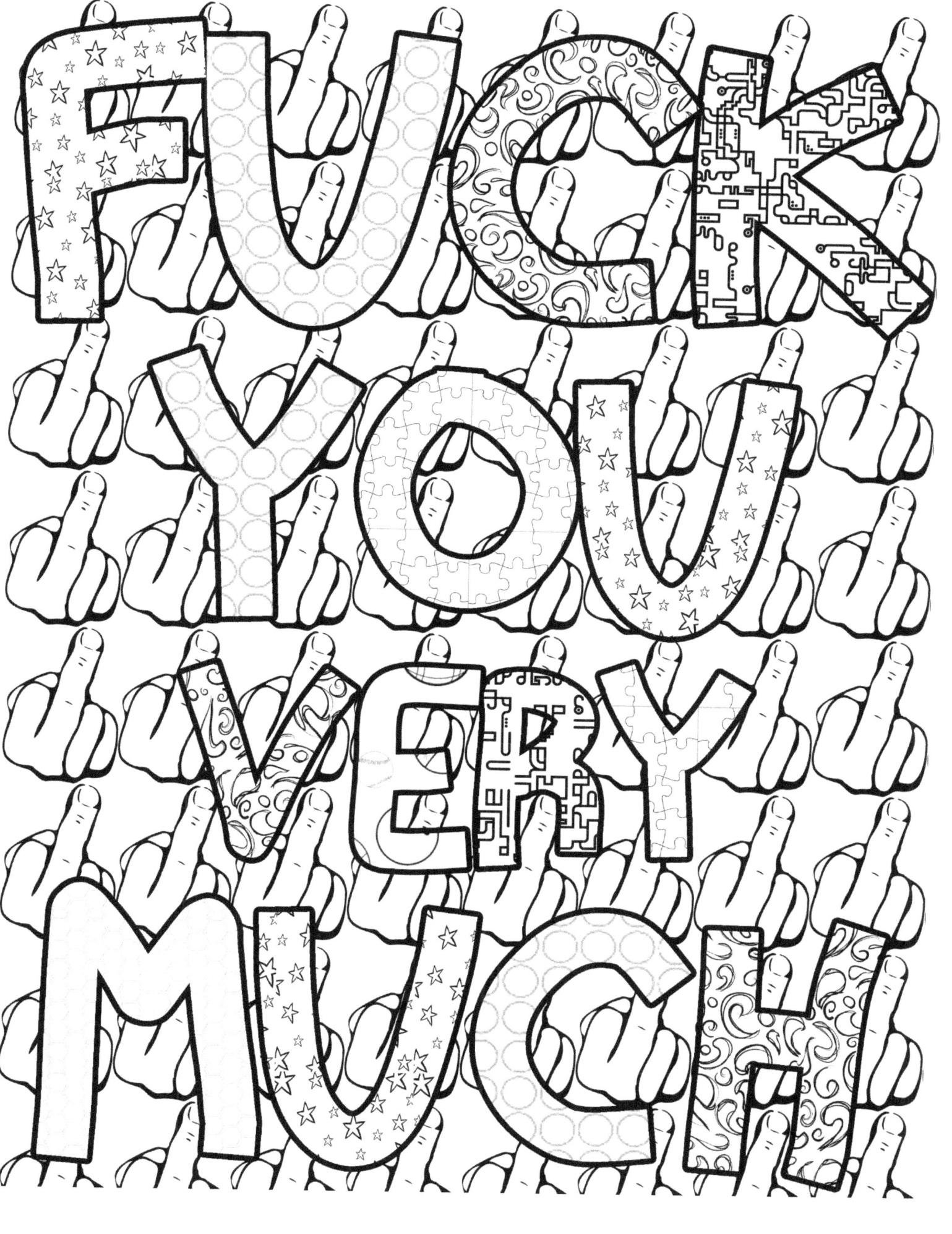

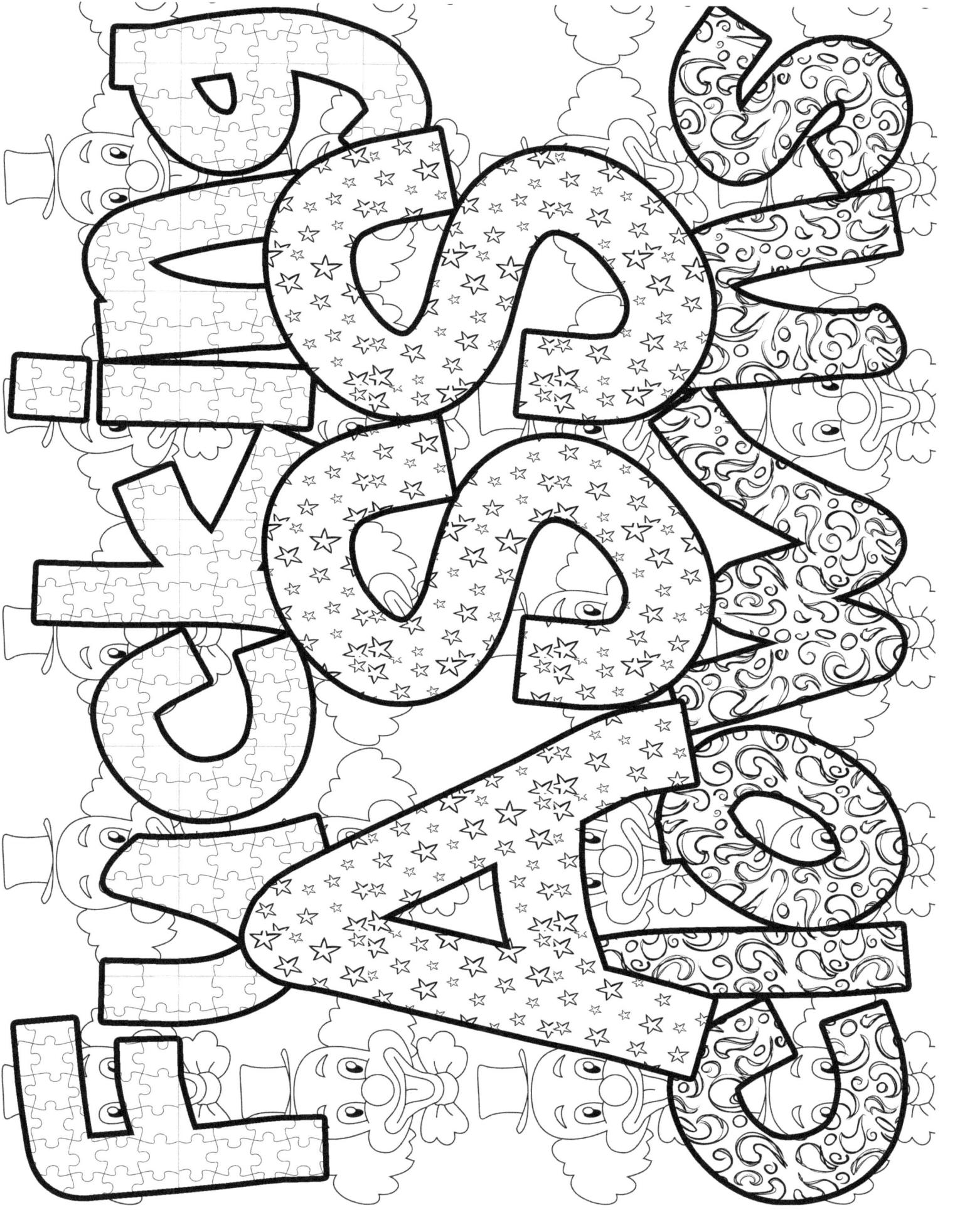

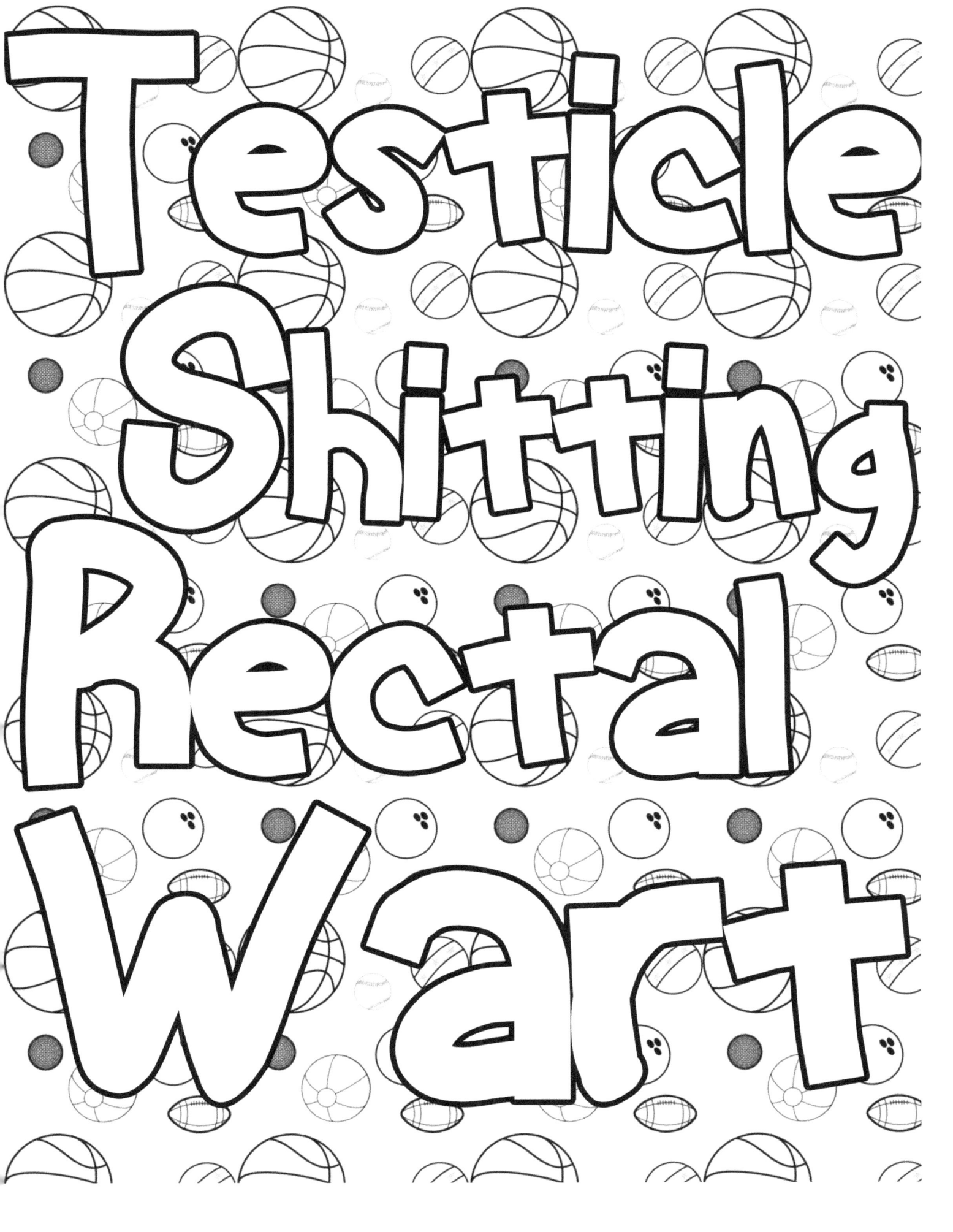

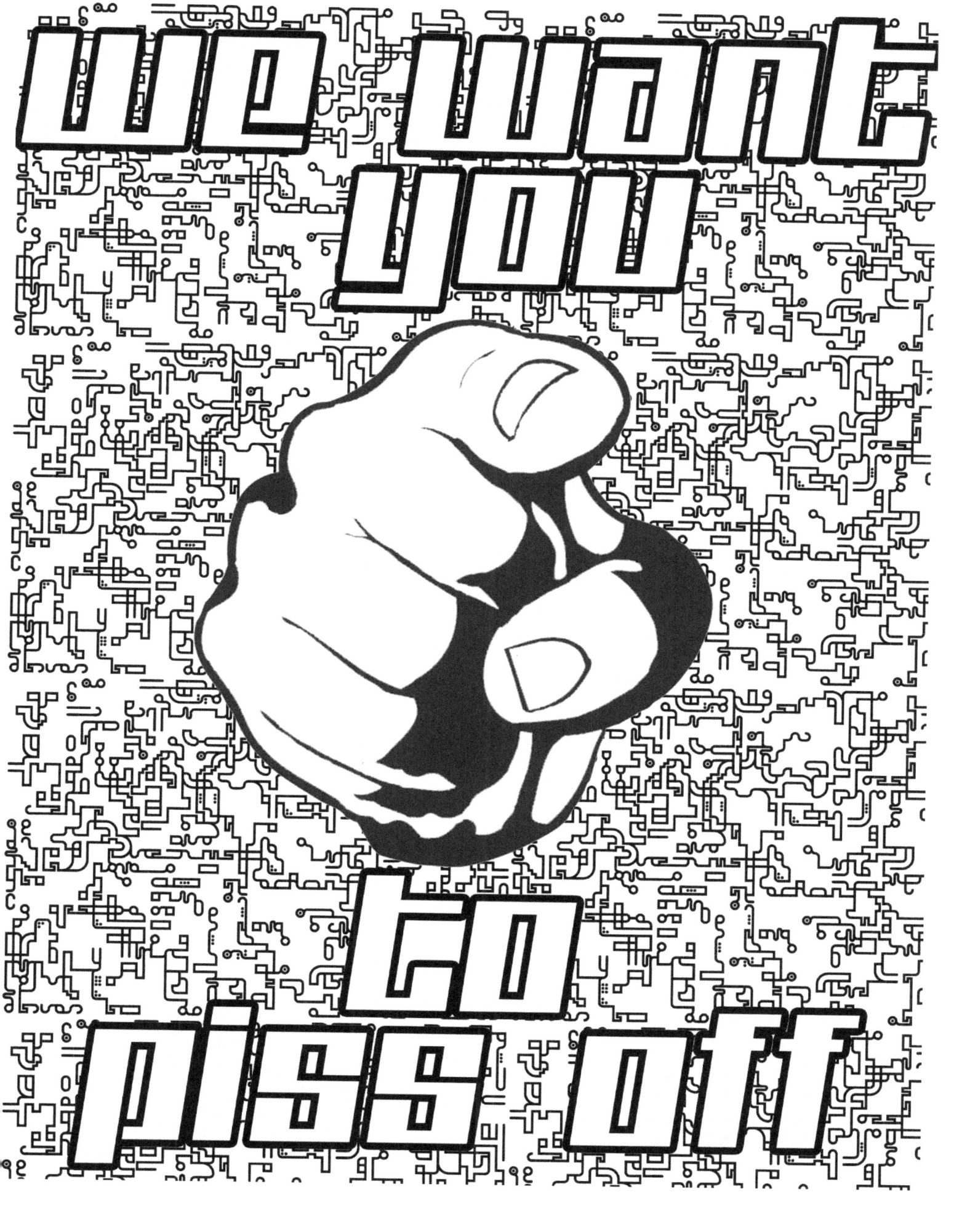

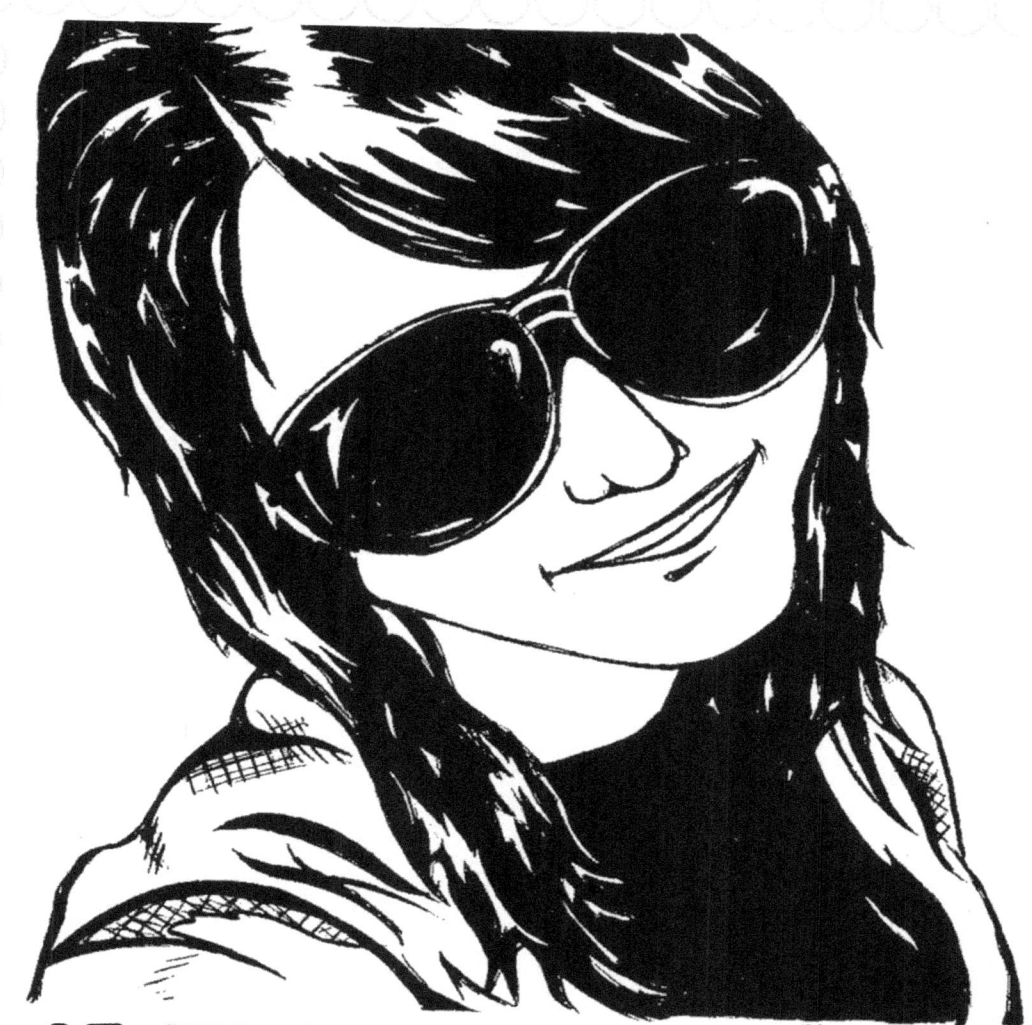

IF IT SOUNDS LIKE A
COMPLIMENT
I'M BEING
SARCASTIC!

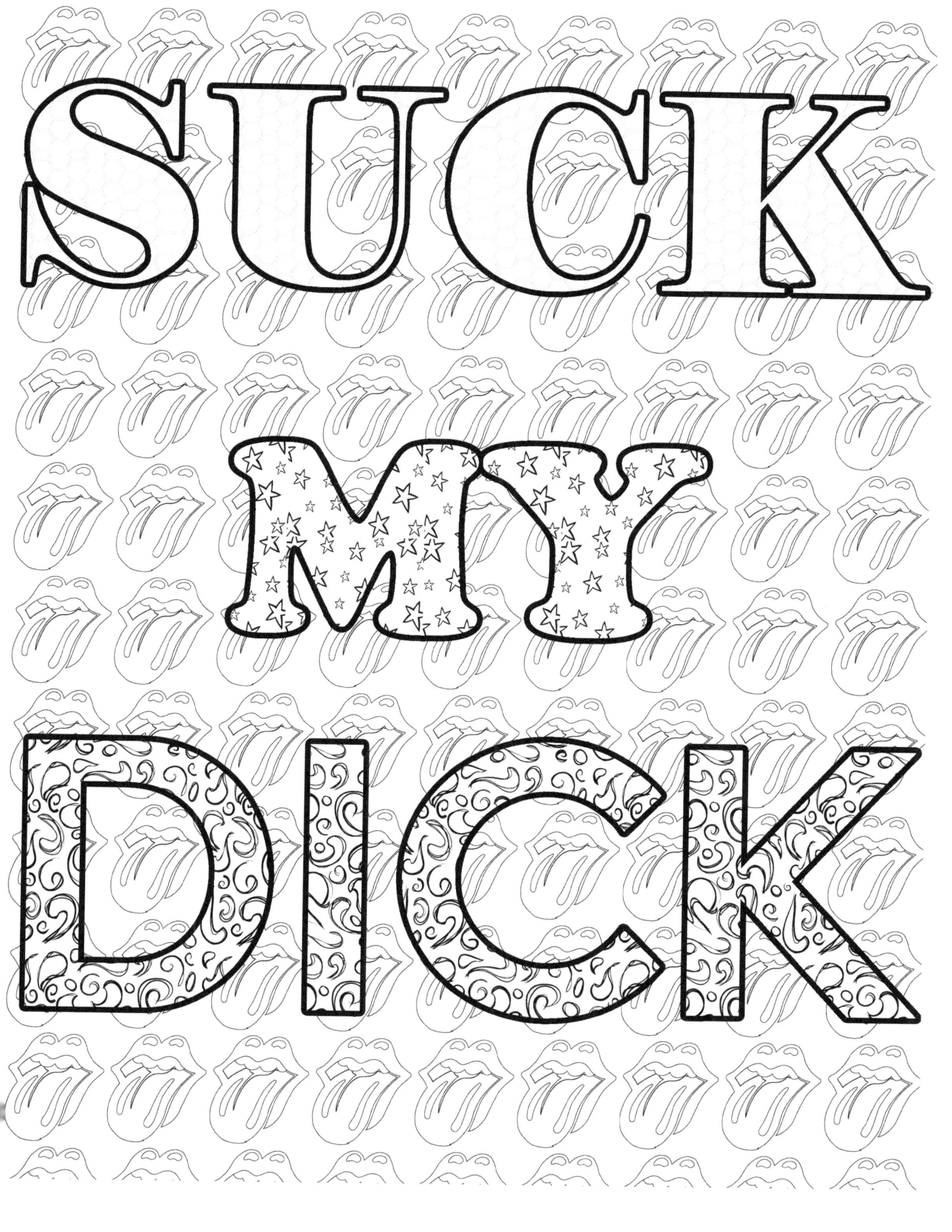

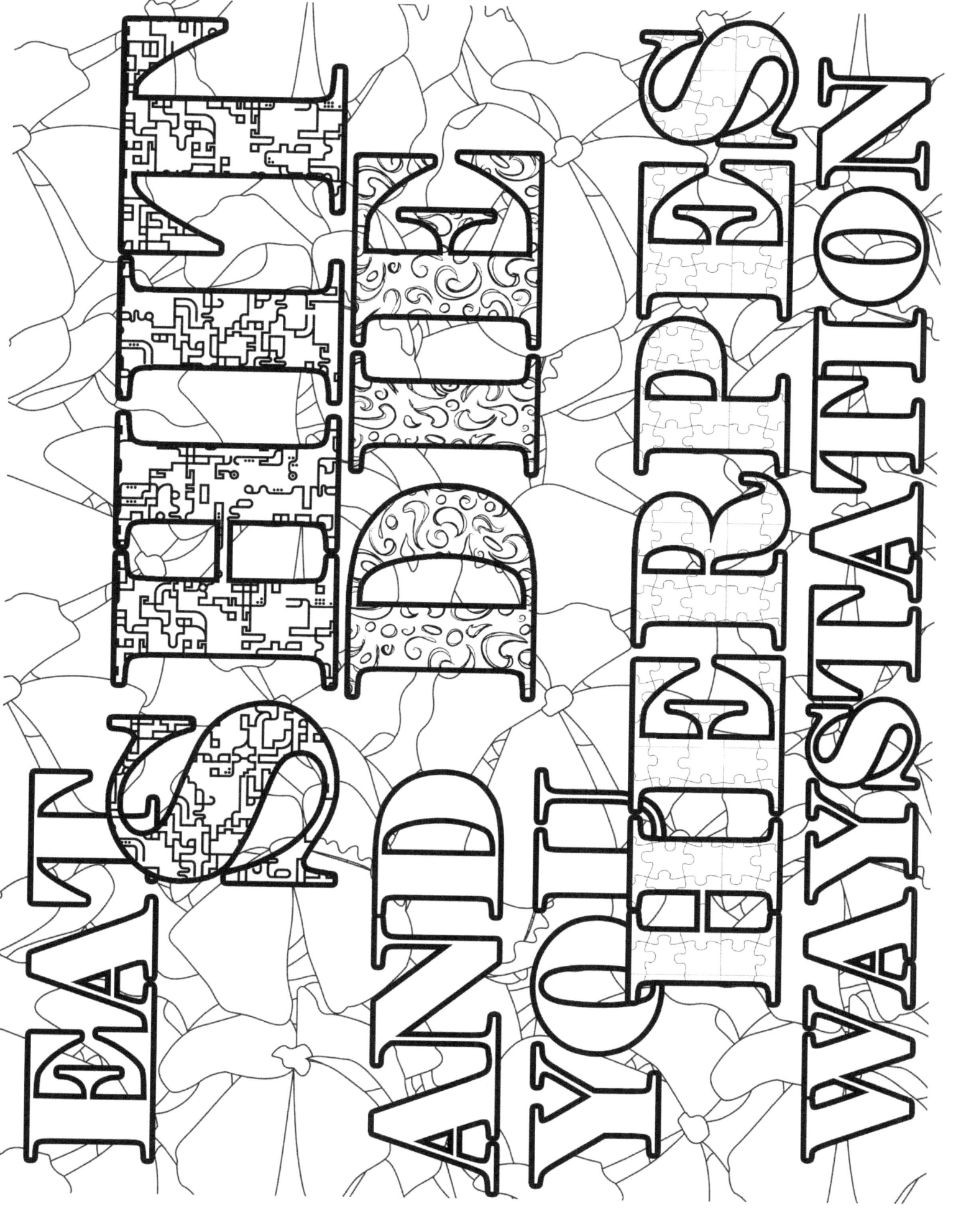

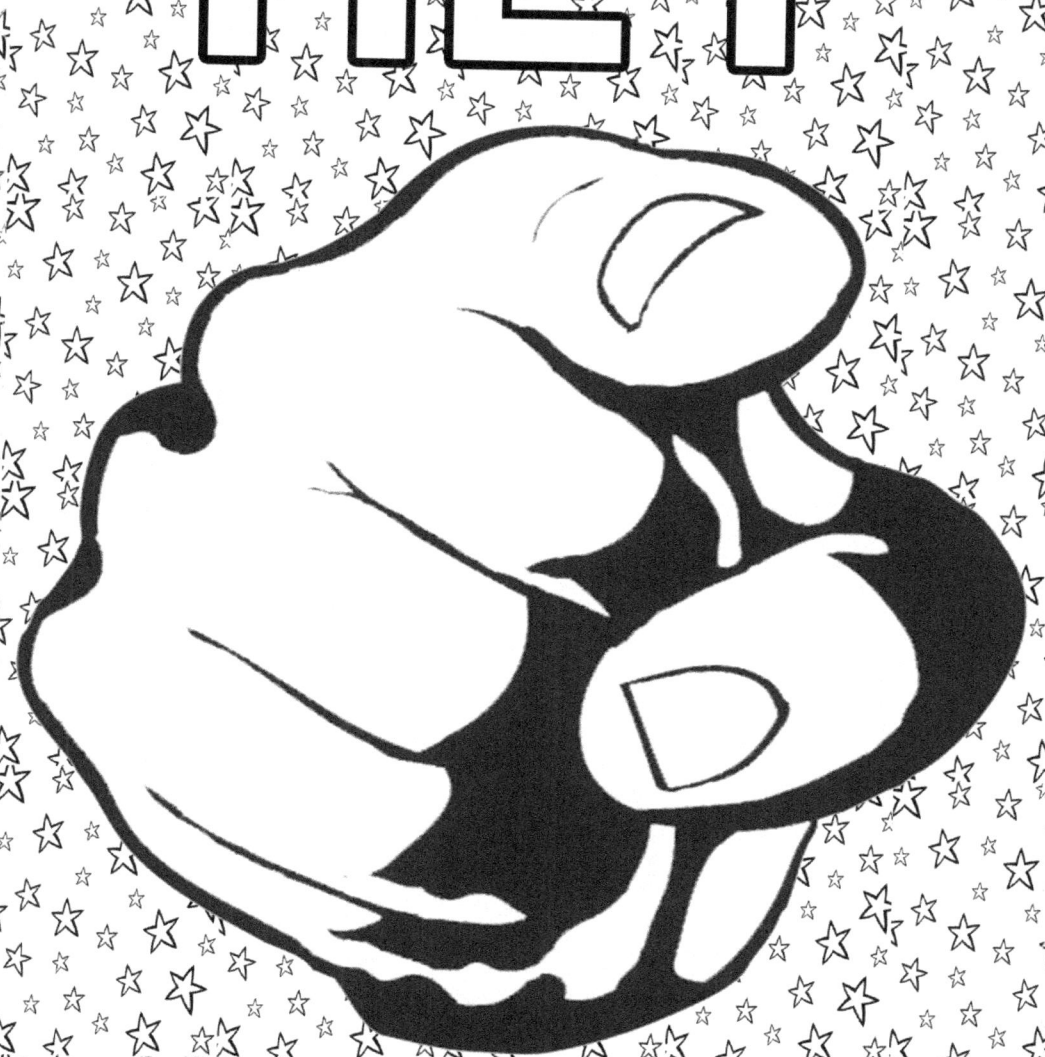

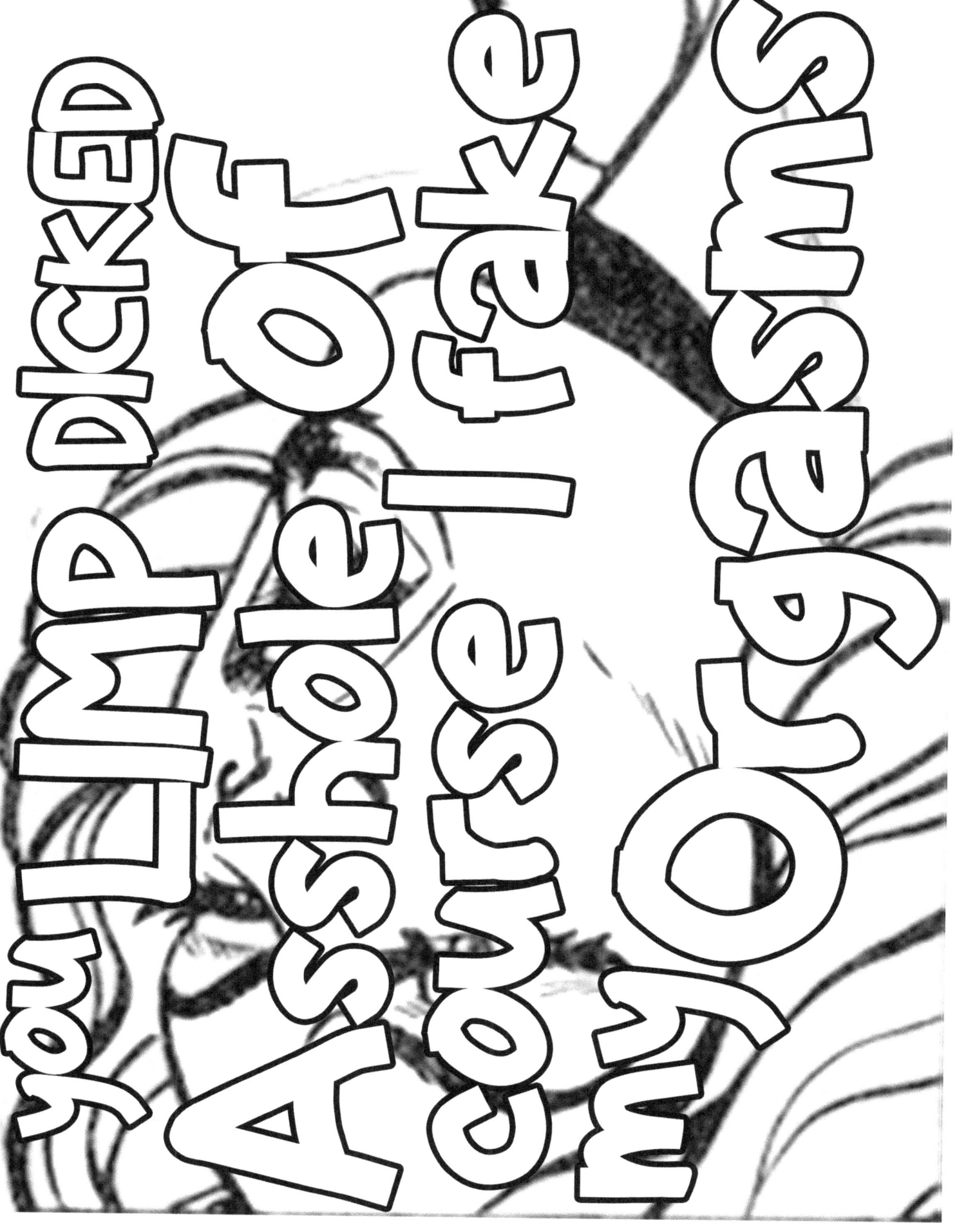

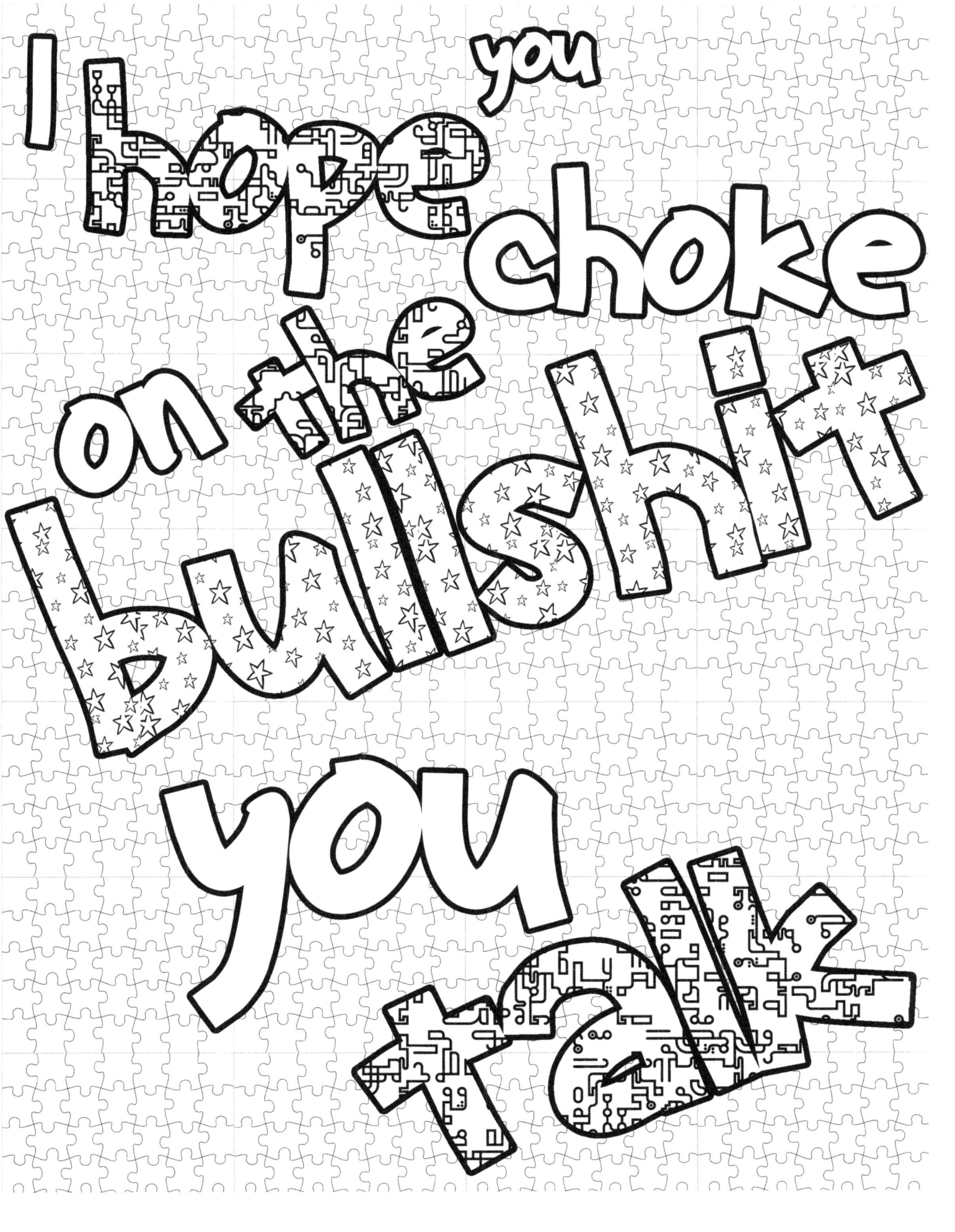

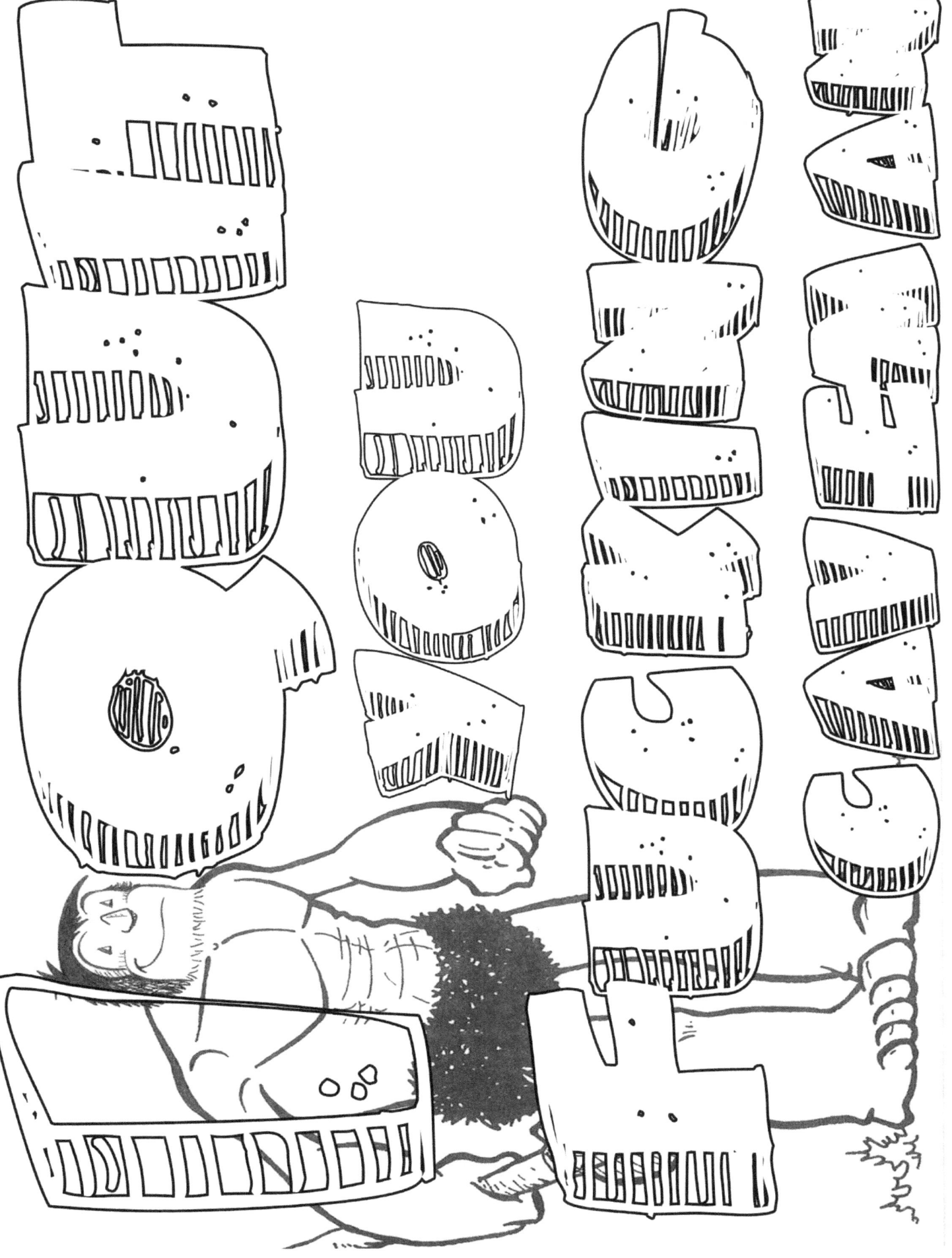

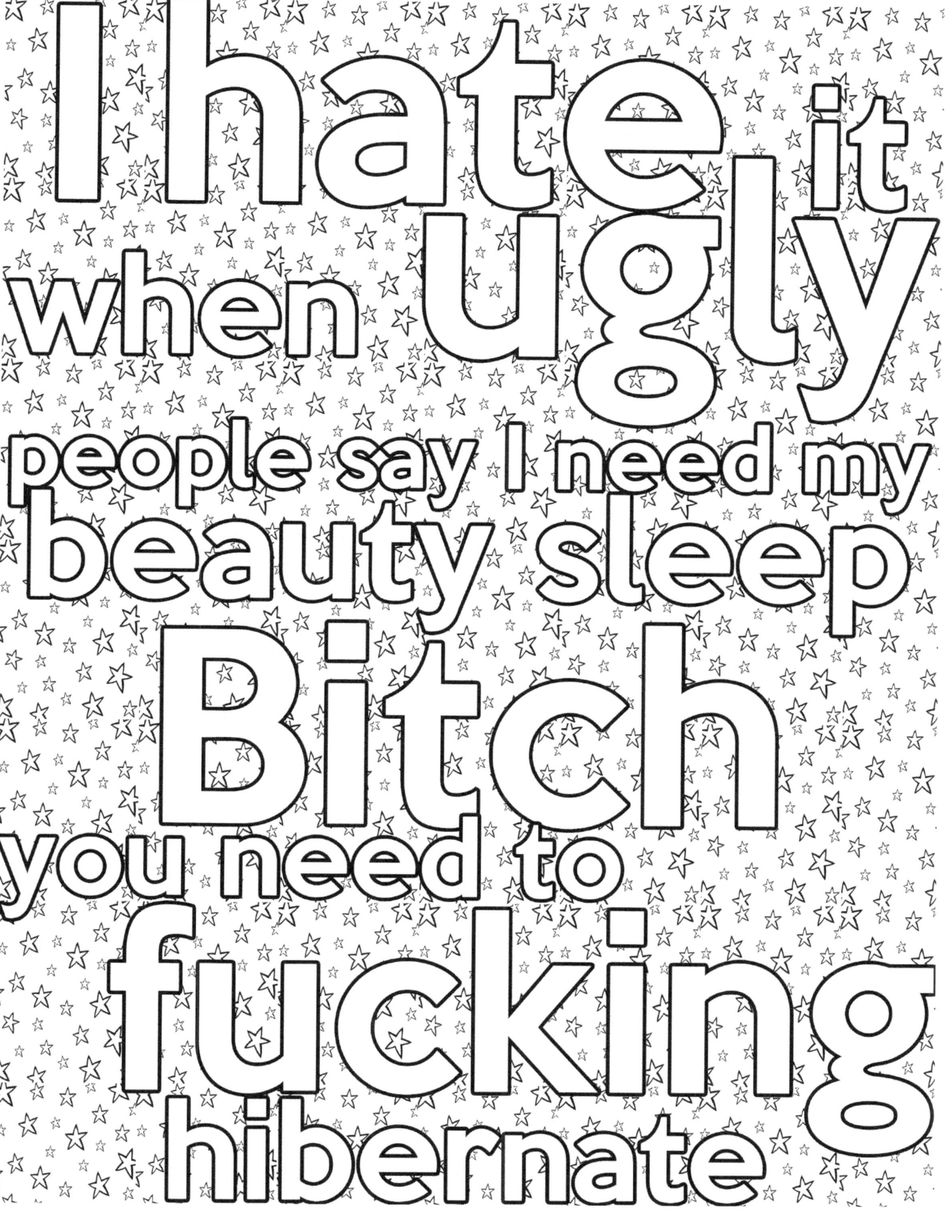

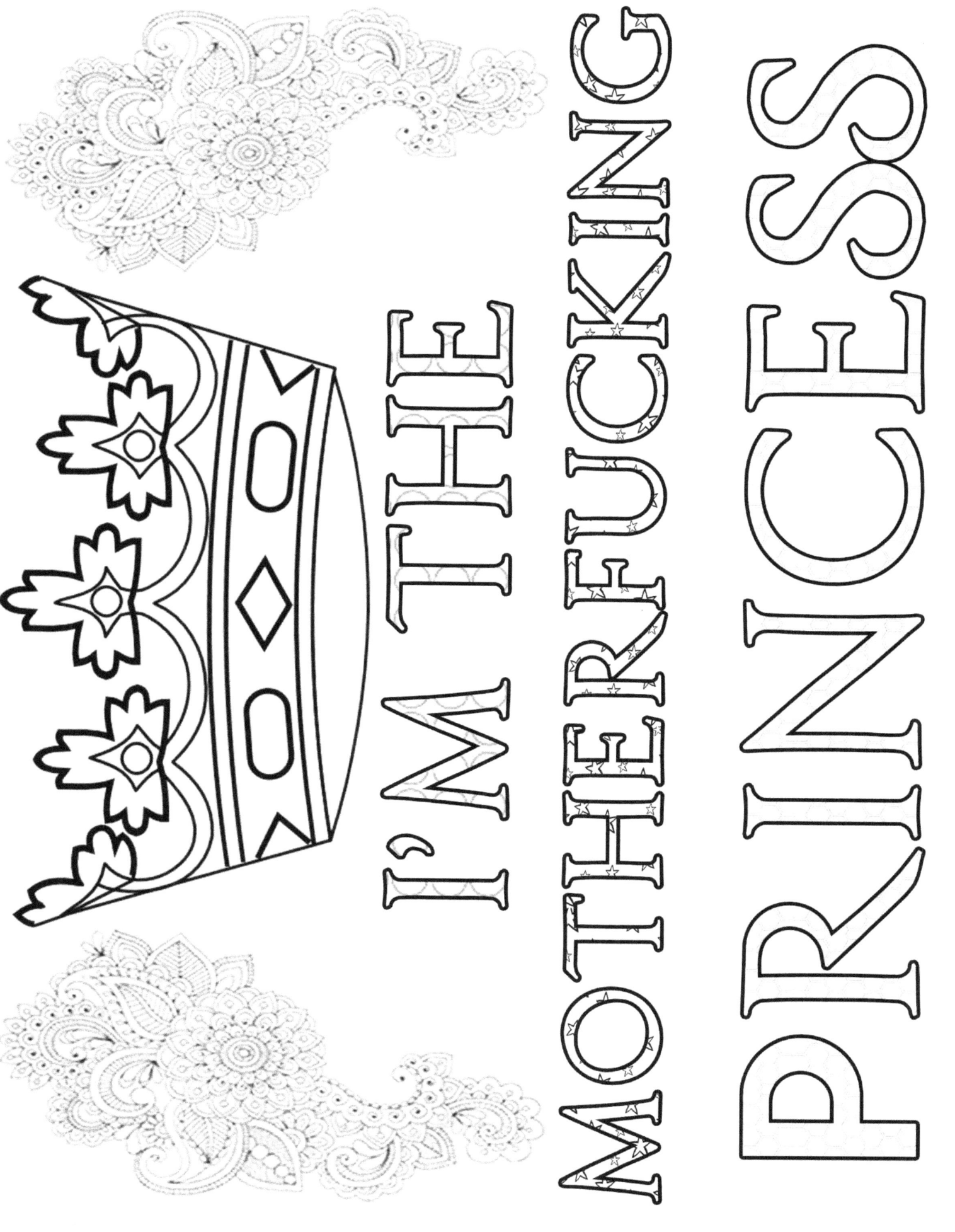

I'M THE MOTHERFUCKING PRINCESS

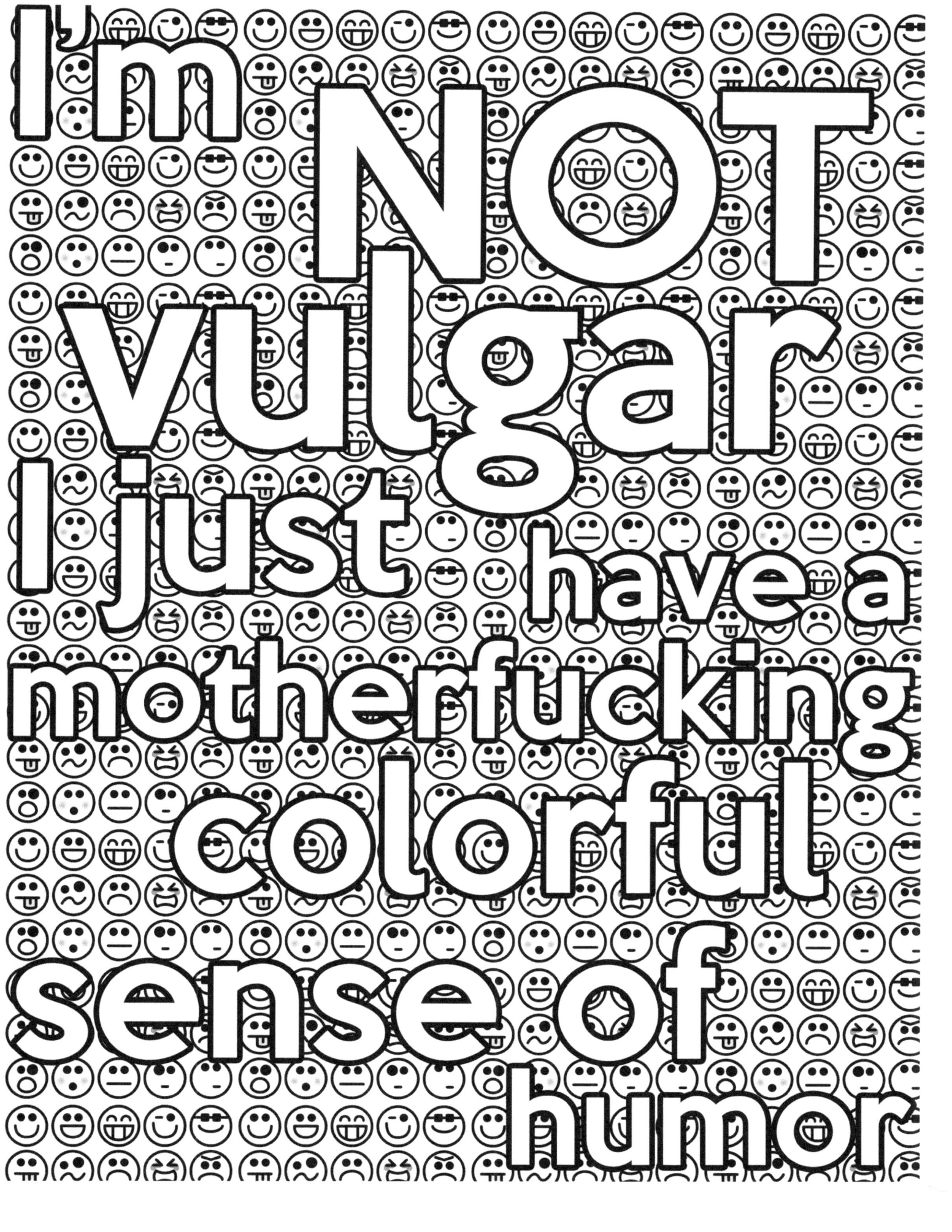

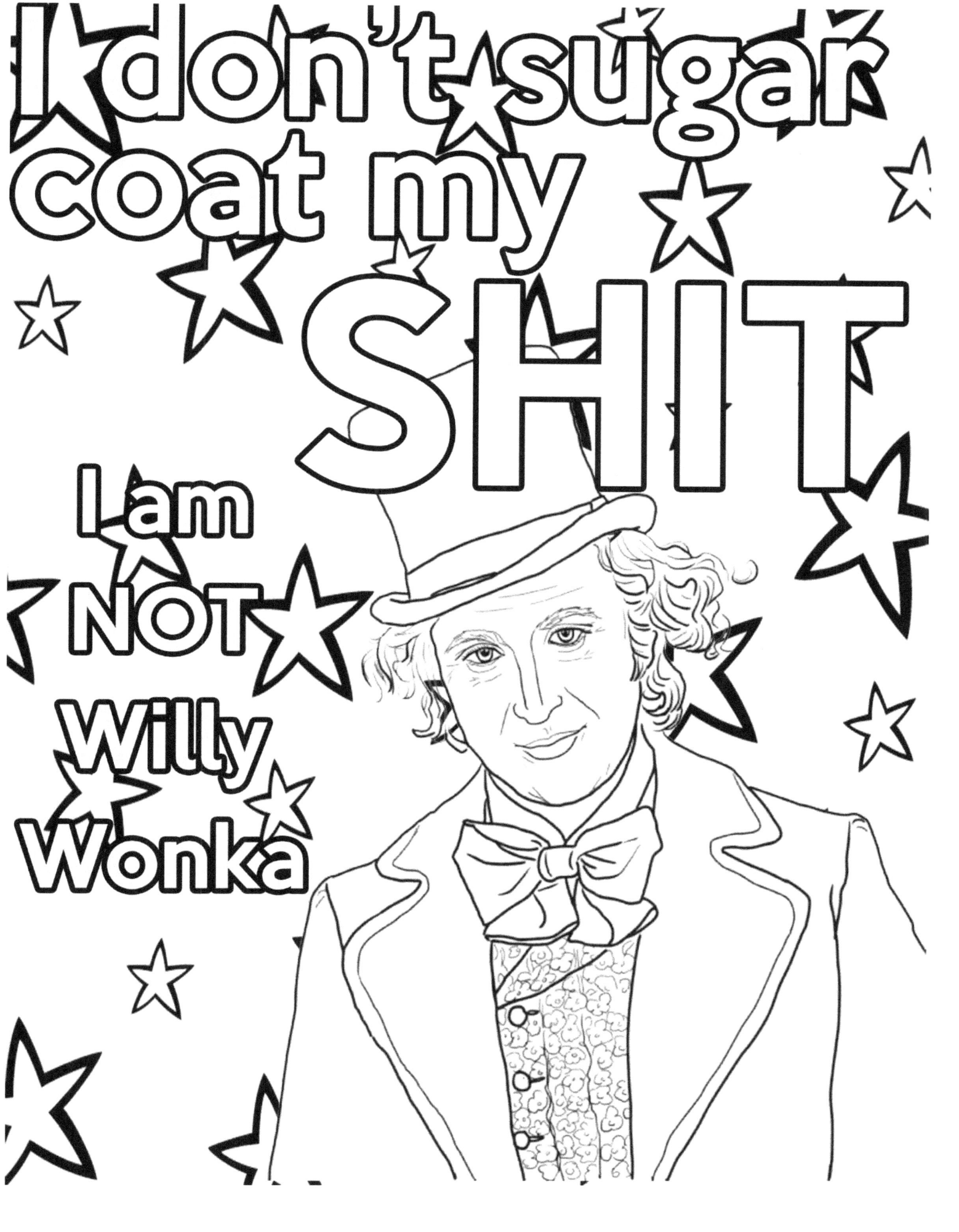

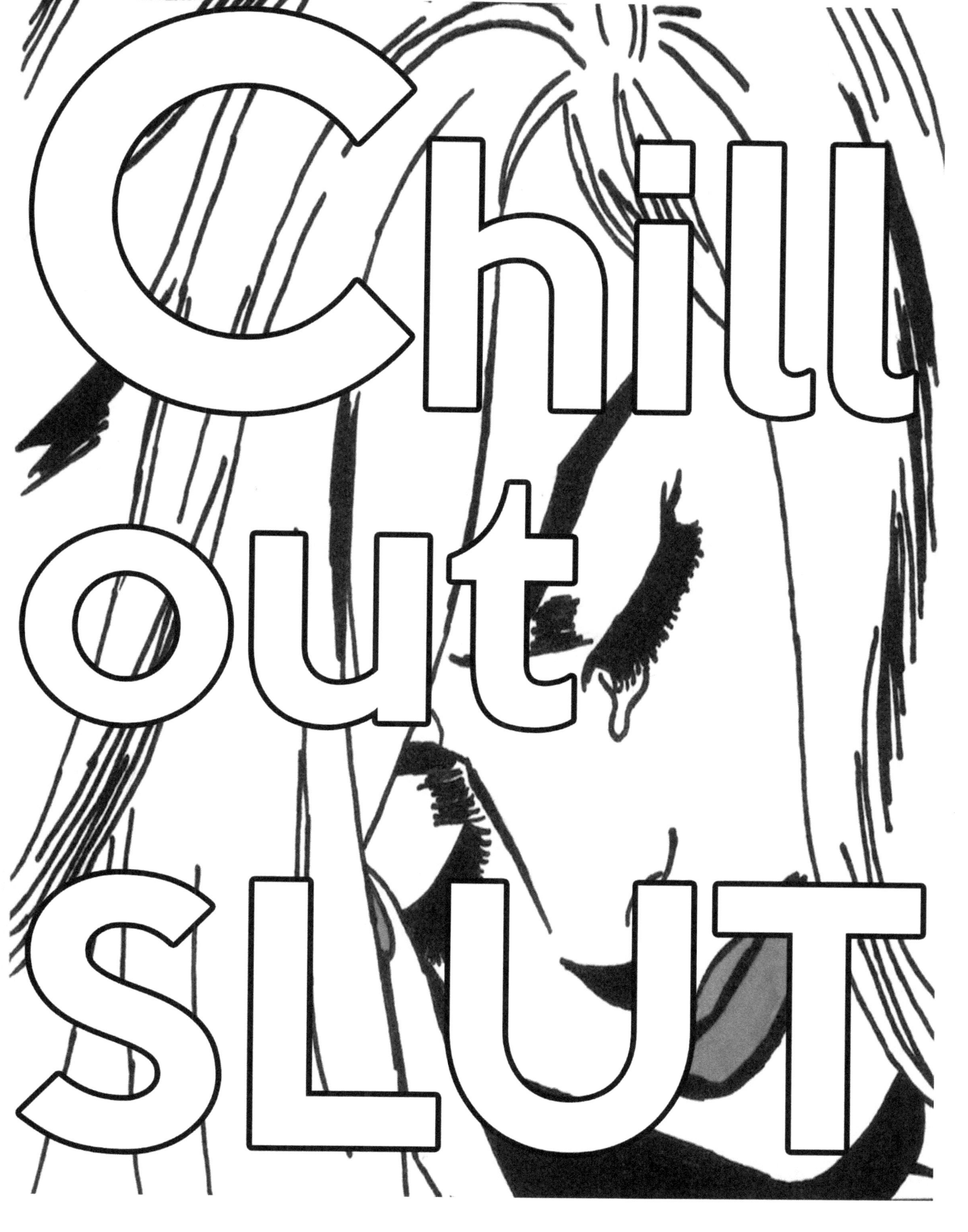

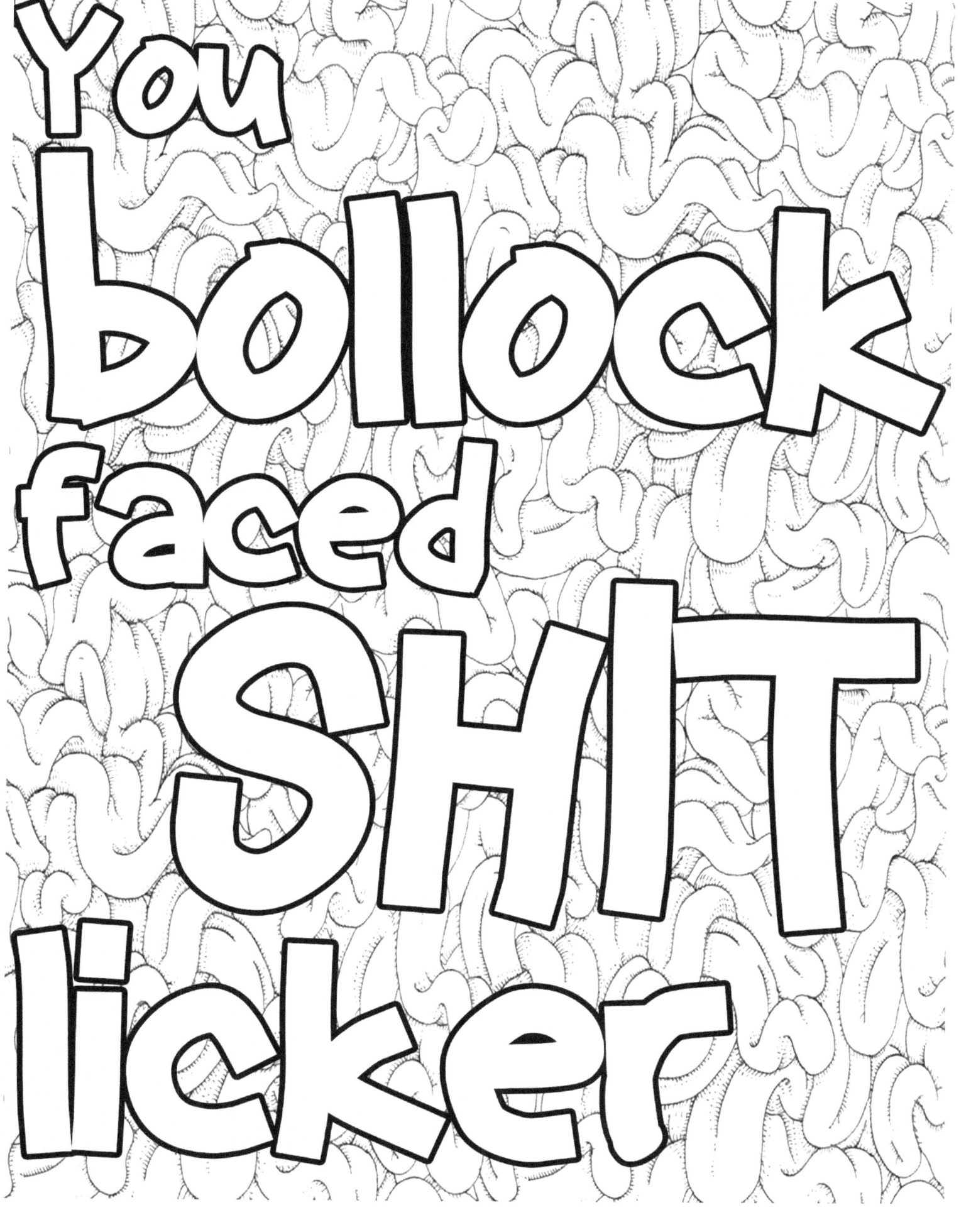

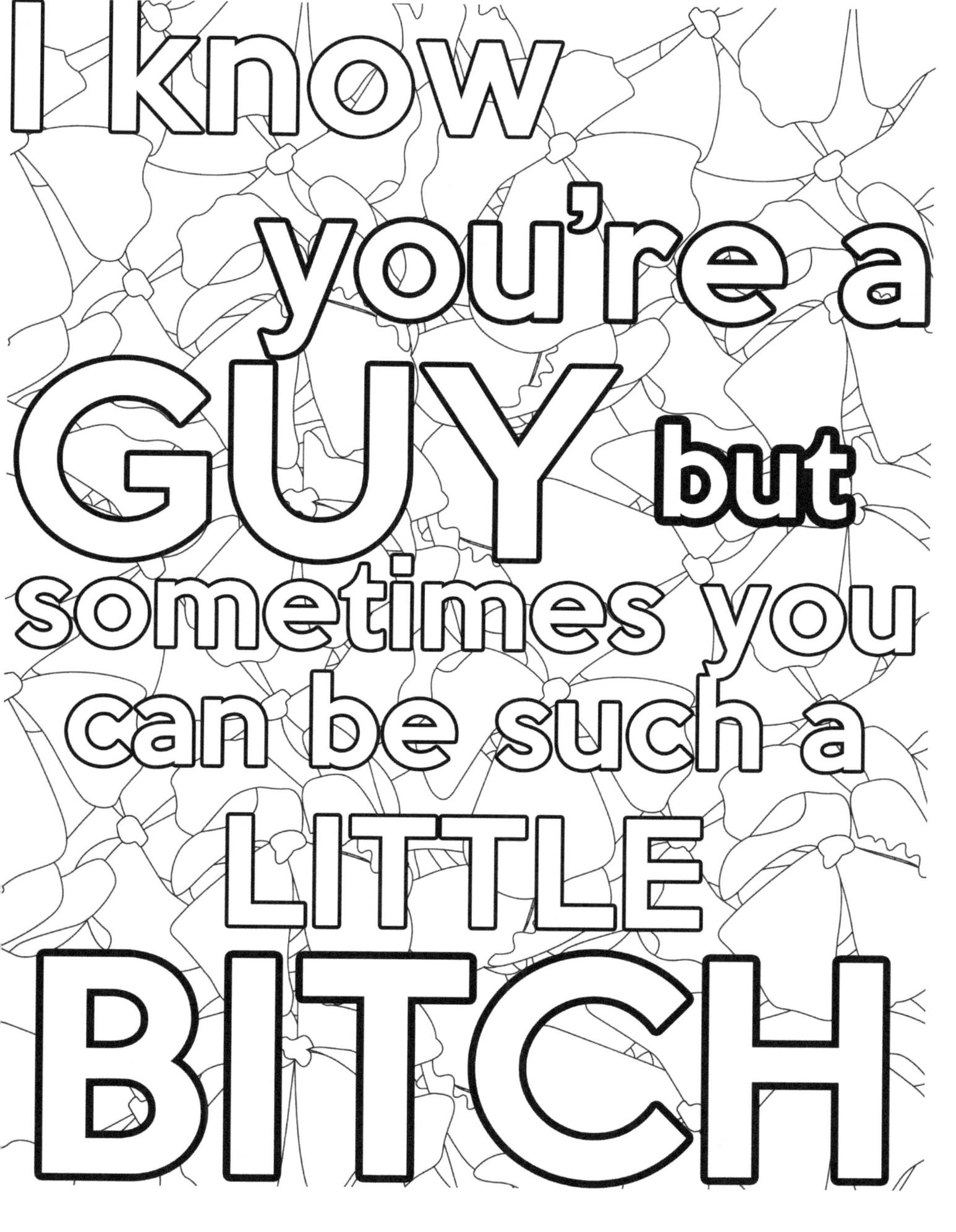

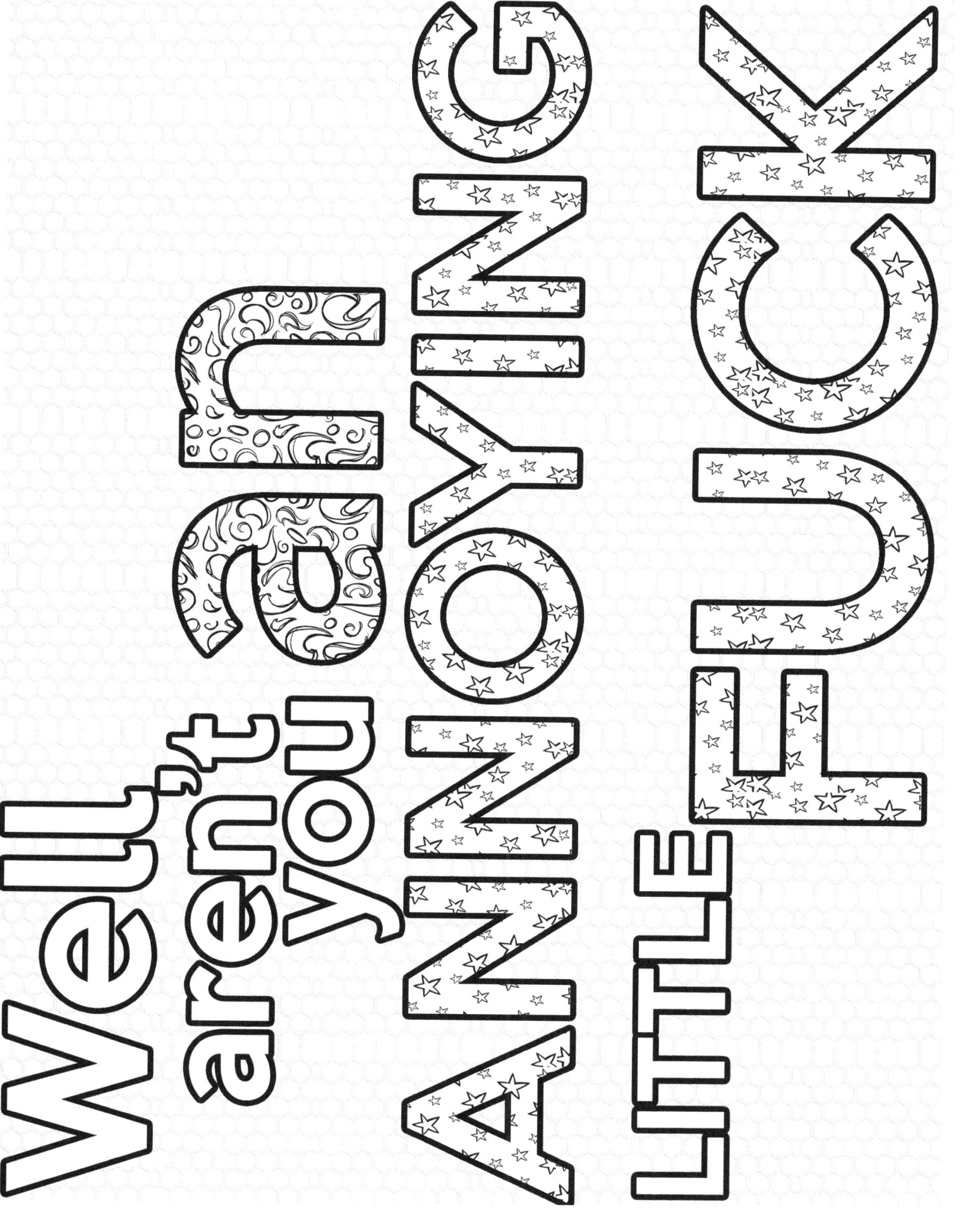

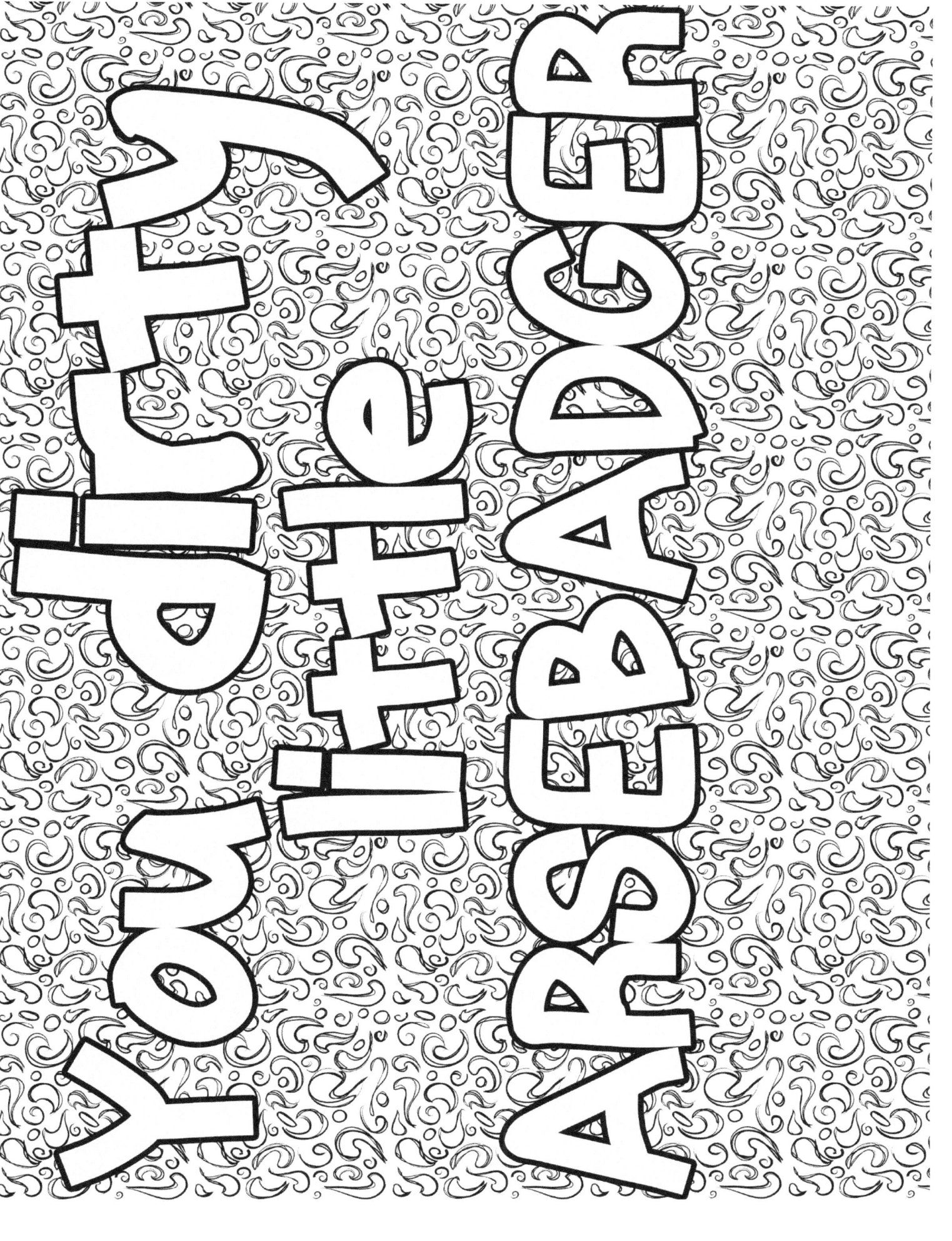

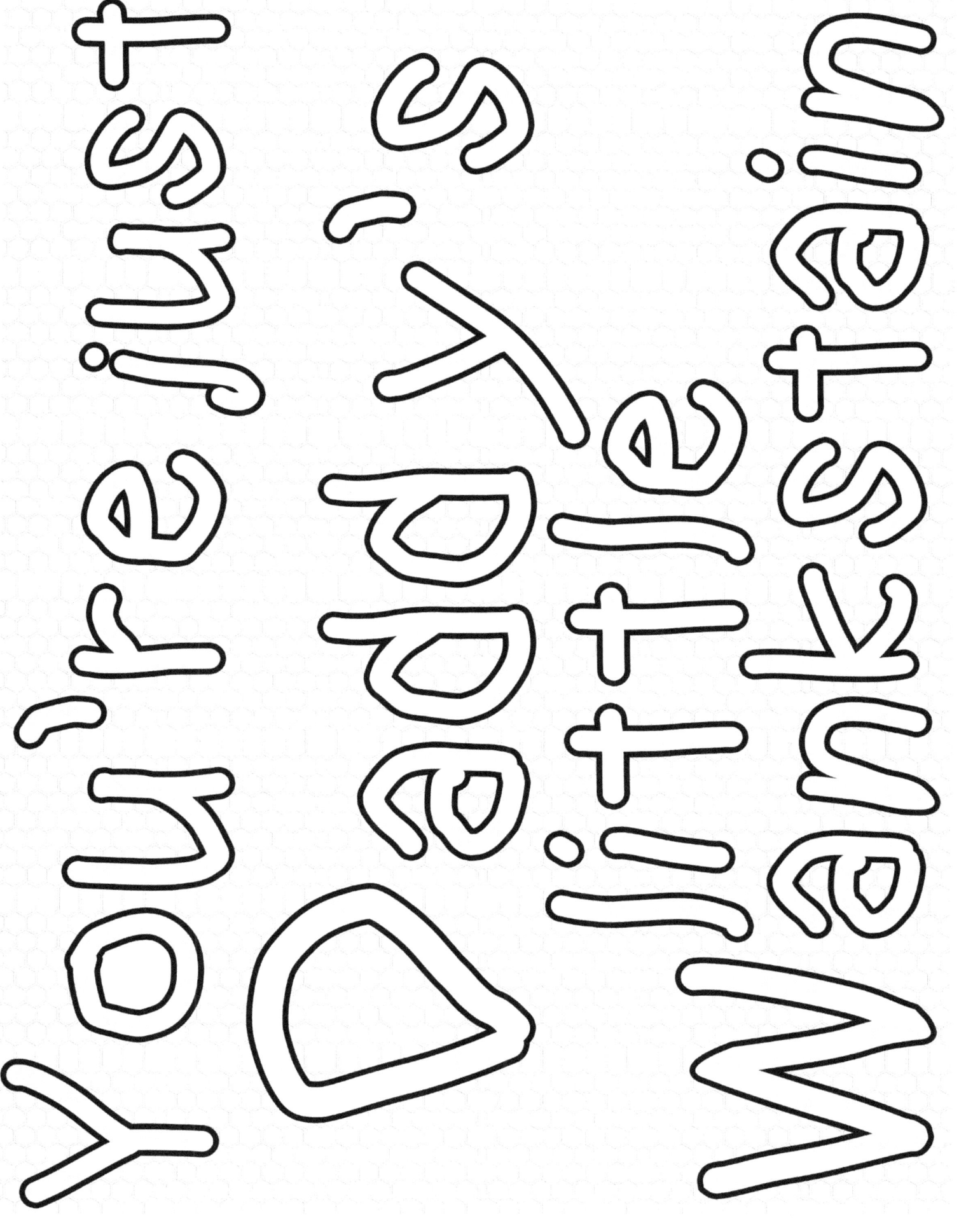

You're just Daddy's little Wankstain

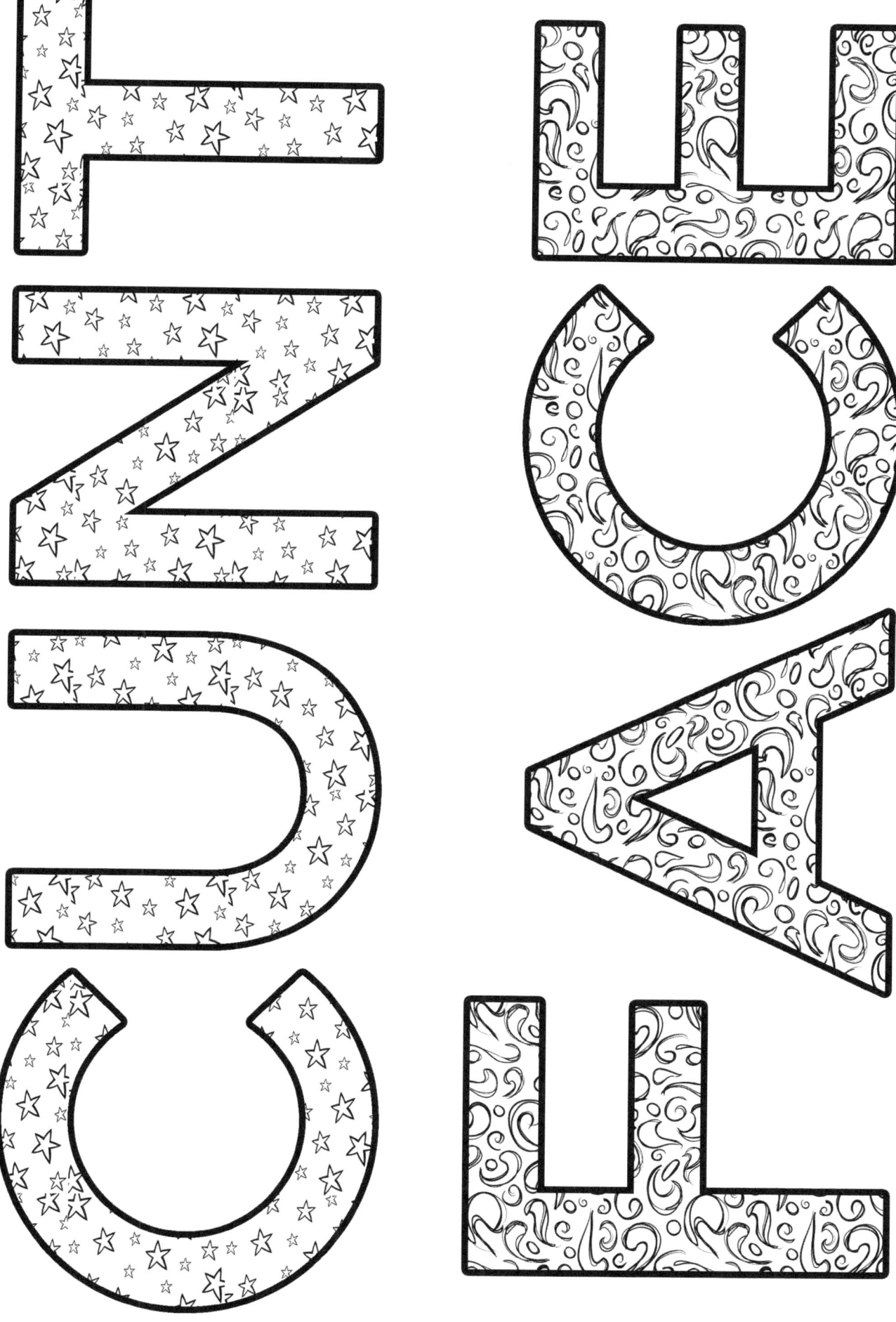

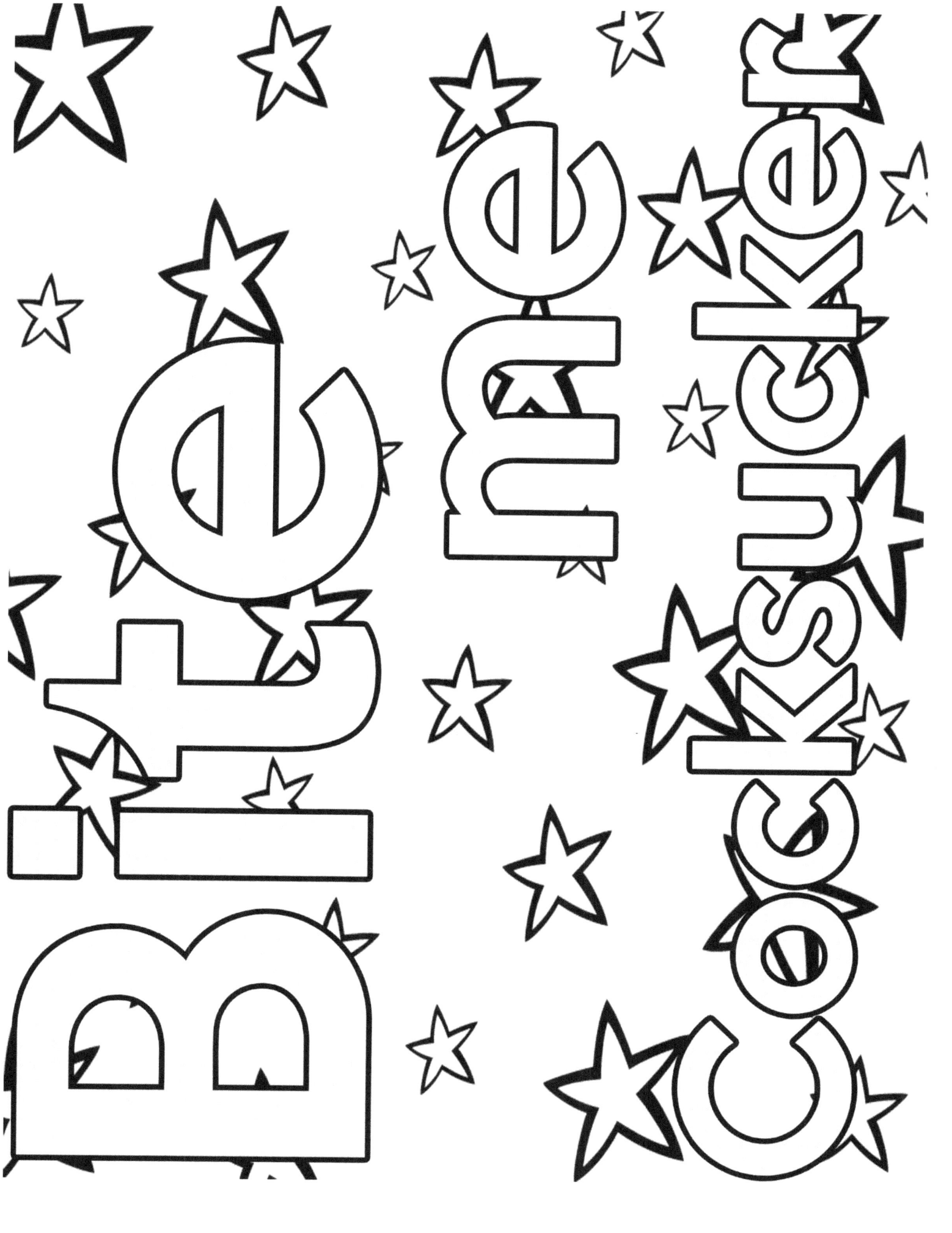

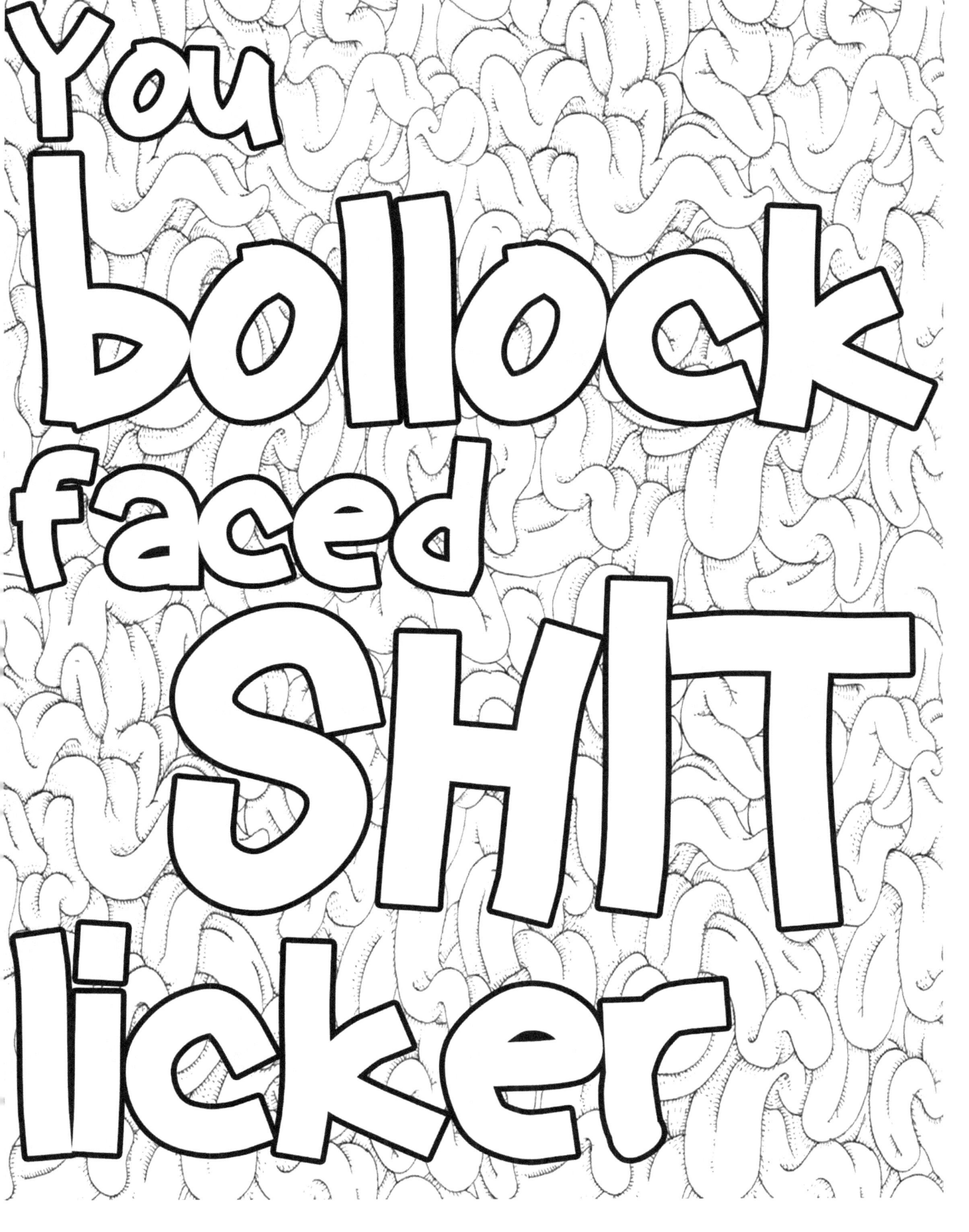

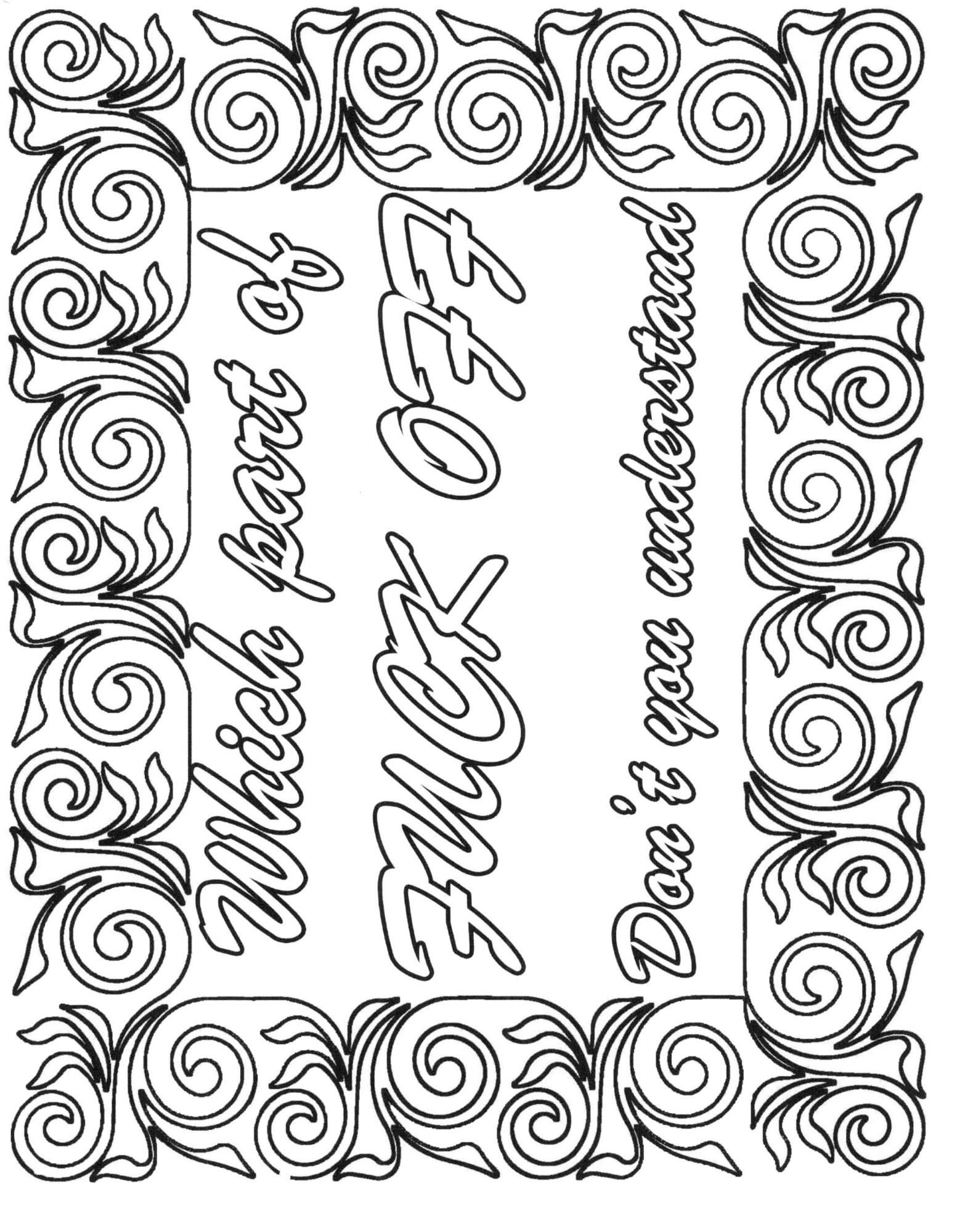